Democracy in Decline?

A *Journal of Democracy* Book
Published under the auspices of the
International Forum for Democratic Studies

Selected Books in the Series
Edited by Larry Diamond and Marc F. Plattner

Democratization and Authoritarianism in the Arab World (2014)

Will China Democratize? (2013)
(with Andrew J. Nathan)

Democracy in East Asia: A New Century (2013)
(with Yun-han Chu)

Liberation Technology: Social Media and the Struggle for Democracy (2012)

Poverty, Inequality, and Democracy (2012)
(with Francis Fukuyama)

Debates on Democratization (2010)

Democratization in Africa: Progress and Retreat (2010)

Democracy: A Reader (2009)

How People View Democracy (2008)

Latin America's Struggle for Democracy (2008)
(with Diego Abente Brun)

The State of India's Democracy (2007)
(with Sumit Ganguly)

Electoral Systems and Democracy (2006)

Assessing the Quality of Democracy (2005)
(Edited by Larry Diamond and Leonardo Morlino)

World Religions and Democracy (2005)
(with Philip J. Costopoulos)

Democracy in Decline?

EDITED BY LARRY DIAMOND AND MARC F. PLATTNER

Foreword by Condoleezza Rice

Johns Hopkins University Press • Baltimore

Printed in the United States of America on acid-free paper
9 8 7 6 5 4 3 2

Johns Hopkins University Press
2715 North Charles Street
Baltimore, Maryland 21218-4363
www.press.jhu.edu

Library of Congress Cataloging-in-Publication Data

Democracy in decline? / edited by Larry Diamond, Marc F. Plattner ;
foreword by Condoleezza Rice.
pages cm. — (A journal of democracy book)
Includes bibliographical references and index.
ISBN 978-1-4214-1818-6 (hardback) — ISBN 978-1-4214-1819-3
(electronic) — ISBN 1-4214-1818-5 (hardcover) 1. Democracy.
2. Democratization. 3. World politics—21st century.
I. Diamond, Larry Jay. II. Plattner, Marc F., 1945–
JC423.D43988 2015
321.8—dc23 2015006239

A catalog record for this book is available from the British Library.

Special discounts are available for bulk purchases of this book. For more information, please contact Special Sales at 410-516-6936 or specialsales@press.jhu.edu.

Johns Hopkins University Press uses environmentally friendly book materials, including recycled text paper that is composed of at least 30 percent post-consumer waste, whenever possible.

CONTENTS

FOREWORD

For the past quarter-century, the *Journal of Democracy* has helped the world to understand the controlled chaos that is democracy. Like the many scholars who have written for the *Journal,* I care deeply about the fate of this system of governance that protects liberty and have studied its ups and downs.

In more recent years, as secretary of state, I found myself defending the proposition that all people should live in freedom and that US policies should reflect that belief. It was not difficult to get agreement to the principle. Yes, it was best if human beings could say what they thought, worship as they pleased, be free from the arbitrary power of the state, and have a say in who would govern them. After all, who would argue that some people should be condemned to live in tyranny?

Yet if one scratched the surface, there was rampant skepticism that democracy is right everywhere, at all times, and for all peoples. One was reminded that cultural explanations once branded Africans as too tribal, Asians too Confucian, and Latin Americans too drawn to *caudillos* to create stable democracies. Those arguments now belong to the past, but a hint of them hangs over the discussion of the events in the Middle East. The Arab Spring has led to disappointment, and democracy seems overmatched by sectarianism, state collapse, and a palpable nostalgia for a more orderly, if authoritarian time.

But it is undeniable that democracy retains its power to appeal to those who do not yet enjoy its benefits. People are willing to face persecution and imprisonment, exile, and even death just for a chance to live a life in liberty, even in the chaotic Middle East.

The authors of the essays in this twenty-fifth anniversary book cannot be accused of indifference to those aspirations. They are some of the strongest advocates for freedom—everywhere and for all people. But they are troubled by what Larry Diamond calls the "democratic recession." The question hangs in the air. Are democracy's best days behind it?

Surely, there are reasons for pessimism, and they are chronicled with precision and insight in the essays that follow. Once-promising democratic transitions have failed, are failing, or remain incomplete. I remember well attending a UN meeting in 2007, as Mali prepared to host the next summit of the Community of Democracies. Just a few years later, Mali fell to a military coup and then descended into open chaos and civil war and was expelled from the organization. But Mali is an object lesson in the ups and downs of democratic transitions. It was readmitted into the Community of Democracies in 2014, even though it is still considered only "partially free."

One can also point to the poor performance of new democracies in delivering even the most basic services—health, jobs, security—for their people. Poor governance is strangling young democracies across the globe and undermining their legitimacy.

And clearly, authoritarian regimes can claim some wins in this regard. China's leadership enjoys legitimacy based on prosperity. Chinese citizens enjoy economic benefits and, in return, forgo political participation. Given the chaos and depravation in so many places, it is a tempting model for others to follow. Similarly, Russia, once thought to be on the verge of joining the liberal-democratic order, has turned back to its authoritarian roots at home and its aggressive policies abroad.

The geopolitical weight of China and Russia threatens to create an international environment that is hostile to democracy. At the same time, those seeking liberty have surely noticed that the United States and Europe have been less vocal in recent years in defending the cause of freedom.

So what should democracy advocates do? Since its first issue, the *Journal* has provided insights on this question for students, scholars, and policymakers alike. The essays in this volume will advance and challenge your thoughts about the prospects of democracy today.

We are reminded that those who believe in the enterprise must find a better way to assist in building state-capacity. We are challenged to find ways to use foreign aid to support efficiency and transparency of young governments. We are cautioned not to think that the long arc of history will inevitably favor freedom.

We can certainly do better in supporting new democratic states and helping them to govern more effectively. But most likely, we will also need to find an abundance of patience. It is not easy for people who have just seized their rights to write rules of the political game that are fair and transparent. It is not easy for majorities to use their newly won freedoms to advocate for the rights of minorities. It is not easy for traditional patriarchal societies to accept the idea that the protection of individual rights must be gender neutral. And it is not easy for people to put aside painful, and often violent, societal divides and learn to trust impartial institutions and the rule of law to resolve differences.

Still, count me as optimistic about democracy's future. Alternatives might earn some temporary legitimacy by providing efficient governance in the short run. But eventually there will be challenges and problems and popular pressure for a different course: That is the authoritarian's nightmare, because—unlike in democracies—there is no peaceful way for the people to change the government.

We must also maintain historical perspective, recognizing the remarkable geographic reach of democracy's march over the past decades. Chile and Colombia, Senegal and Ghana, Japan, South Korea, and Indonesia have given an answer to those who thought that democracy could take root only where Europe's Enlightenment had prepared the ground.

And Americans, of all people, should be patient. The odds were surely long that the descendants of slaves would win their rights through appeal to the US Constitution that once counted their ancestors as three-fifths of a man. That is a recent development, of course. We have just celebrated fifty years since Selma and the Voting Rights Act, marking the United States' second democratic transition.

So, while those of us who are lucky enough to live in freedom have the right to question its promise, we should not forget that people who do not yet enjoy its benefits still seem determined to win it. That is the greatest reason for optimism that democracy is not permanently in decline. And it is a call to redouble our commitment to the proposition that no one should live in tyranny—even if the road ahead is hard and long.

—Condoleezza Rice

ACKNOWLEDGMENTS

This volume had its origins in the twenty-fifth anniversary issue of the *Journal of Democracy*, published in January 2015. Most of the articles in that issue addressed the theme, "Is Democracy in Decline?" Some discussed this question in a global context, while others focused on a particular country or region. Even before the issue appeared, Greg Britton, the editorial director of Johns Hopkins University Press (JHUP), had suggested to us the idea of collecting the globally oriented essays in a short book. We responded positively to Greg's idea, and he quickly set about drawing up plans for the volume's production.

Our intention to go forward with this book project was confirmed at the *Journal of Democracy*'s twenty-fifth anniversary celebration, held on January 29 at the Hotel Monaco in Washington, DC. This event featured a panel discussion, attended by more than 200 people, on the very question that provides this volume's title. The participants included five of the contributors to this book—Thomas Carothers, Larry Diamond, Steven Levitsky, Marc Plattner, and Lucan Way—as well as Alina Mungiu-Pippidi (who had contributed a regionally focused essay on the postcommunist world to the January 2015 issue of the *Journal*.) The lively and impassioned debate at the panel and the enthusiastic audience reaction suggested that there would be keen interest among a wider circle of readers in a book on the subject.

We wish to express our deep gratitude to our colleagues at Johns Hopkins University Press: to Greg Britton for inspiring and championing this project and to managing editor Juliana McCarthy, also of the Books Division, for her efficient shepherding of this volume through the production process; and also to the Journals Division, which generously helped to fund the twenty-fifth anniversary event and whose head, Bill Breichner, offered some gracious remarks at the reception. Our longstanding collaboration with JHUP has been as congenial as it has been productive.

We also owe a huge debt to our parent organization, the National Endowment for Democracy. The Endowment's president, Carl Gershman, and its Board of Directors, currently chaired by former Representative Martin Frost, have never wavered in their support of the *Journal,* while completely respecting our editorial independence and integrity. We count ourselves extremely fortunate to have the privilege of functioning within such an admirable and open-minded institution. We also want to thank the *Journal*'s other funders over the years, especially the Lynde and Harry Bradley Foundation, which provided us with financial support for more than two decades.

Credit for the success of the *Journal*'s twenty-fifth anniversary celebration goes in large measure to our colleagues at NED's International Forum for Democratic Studies, under the leadership of executive director Christopher Walker. Special praise is due senior research and conferences officer Melissa Aten, whose perseverance and assiduous attention to detail made the organization of this complex event appear deceptively easy.

Above all, we want to thank the *Journal*'s superb and seasoned staff. Each one of the essays that follow was improved by the editorial handiwork of executive editor Phil Costopoulos (who has been with us since the *Journal*'s founding) or of senior editor Tracy Brown. Managing editor Brent Kallmer did his usual splendid job of dealing with the challenges of layout and production, and assistant editor Hilary Collins, a relative newcomer, has already proven herself a valuable member of the editorial team. Their contributions to the *Journal*, to previous *Journal of Democracy* books, and to this volume in particular have been absolutely indispensable.

—Marc F. Plattner and Larry Diamond

DEMOCRACY IN DECLINE?

INTRODUCTION

MARC F. PLATTNER

Is democracy in decline? Certainly, the perception that it is in decline has become more widespread than at any time during the past quarter-century. This is not a casual observation on my part. Having served as the coeditor of the *Journal of Democracy* since it published its inaugural issue in January 1990, I have regularly devoted my attention to tracking democracy's advances and setbacks around the world. For more than 25 years, my coeditor Larry Diamond and I have been "taking the temperature" of democracy. Since 1998, we have published annually an article summarizing Freedom House's survey *Freedom in the World*, and we have featured numerous other essays analyzing democracy's global trajectory, beginning with Samuel P. Huntington's classic 1991 article introducing the concept of the "third wave" of democratization.

So when we needed to choose a theme for the *Journal*'s twenty-fifth anniversary issue, it was perhaps only to be expected that we would once again focus on the subject of democracy's global standing. Some of the *Journal*'s readers, however, were surely surprised to see as the headline on this special issue "Is Democracy in Decline?" For a journal that is unabashedly in favor of democracy, weighing the evidence of its decline obviously was not the kind of celebratory theme that might have been preferred for marking a historic milestone. Yet this seemed to be the question that everyone was asking as 2015 approached, and we decided to pose it to the contributors to our anniversary issue. The interest generated by our special issue convinced us that we had made the right choice, and we have now gathered its essays with a global focus in the volume that you have before you: *Democracy in Decline?*

Tracing the viewpoints and opinions expressed in the *Journal* over the years (especially on its five-year anniversaries) gives one a good sense of the way in which evaluations of and sentiments about the state of democracy have evolved since 1990. The editors' introduction that Larry Diamond and I wrote for the inaugural issue was animated by the view that democracy was experiencing a "remarkable worldwide resurgence" but also by a concern that it still lagged behind its rivals with respect to political ideas and organization. Five eventful years later, we recognized both that democracy had spread to many more countries and that it had made huge improvements in terms of ideas and organization. We asserted that democracy had "gained enormous ground" with respect to "international legitimacy" and that it now "reign[ed] supreme in the ideological sphere." Multilateral organizations were increasingly endorsing democratic principles, and a whole new field of international democracy assistance had emerged. At the turn of the century, these trends seemed only to be growing stronger. In introducing a special tenth-anniversary issue on democracy in the world, modeled on Alexis de Tocqueville's *Democracy in America,* we argued that Tocqueville had supplanted Marx, and we concluded, "We are all Tocquevilleans now."

By 2005, however, our tone had grown far more downbeat, and we acknowledged a darkening mood among supporters of democracy. We attributed this in part to the travails of democracy-building in post-invasion Iraq and to Russia's descent back into authoritarianism, but we argued that the overall global trends were mixed and did not justify discouragement among democrats. By 2010, we were prepared to grant that "there now may even be grounds for speaking of an erosion of freedom over the past few years, though its dimensions are very slight."

CONFRONTING DECLINE

Yet now in 2015, as this volume reflects, we have felt compelled to confront head-on the question of whether democracy is in decline. Why? There are two aspects to the answer, which, although intertwined, are in some measure separable. The first deals with what is actually taking place on the ground: How many countries are democratic? Is their number rising or falling? What is the situation with respect to such crucial liberal-democratic features as freedom of the press, rule of law, free and fair elections, and the like? The second, more subjective aspect concerns the standing of democracy in the world: how is it viewed in terms of legitimacy and attractiveness? It is in this latter dimension that the evidence, or at least the widespread perception, of decline is most striking.

As readers will see, the first dimension is open to differing interpretations. The divergence among them is most sharply posed by comparing Steven Levitsky and Lucan Way's chapter, "The Myth of Democratic Recession," with Larry Diamond's chapter, "Facing Up to the Democratic Recession." Levitsky and Way point out that even the Freedom House data show only a very slight decline in levels of freedom since 2000 and that other indices show none at all. In addition, they argue that during the 1990s most observers (including Freedom House) were too prone to count any country where an autocratic regime fell as a case of transition to democracy. In the view of Levitsky and Way, many of these countries temporarily enjoyed "pluralism by default" because of authoritarian weakness, but they never truly established democracy. Many of them have now seen a consolidation of authoritarianism, but because their regimes were wrongly classified as democratic in the first place, this should not be seen as evidence of democratic decline.

Larry Diamond, while not necessarily disputing Levitsky and Way's criticism of how these countries were rated in the early 1990s, finds other empirical evidence that the past decade has been "a period of at least incipient decline in democracy." He cites an increasing incidence of democratic breakdowns, the poor performance of new democracies according to various measures of good governance and the rule of law, and democratic backsliding or stagnation in the biggest and wealthiest non-Western countries. There are strong arguments on both sides of this debate, but ultimately I do not think that analyses of the Freedom House (or other) numbers can settle the larger question.

Moreover, the broad contours of the trends revealed by the data are not really in dispute. Democracy began to make significant gains in the world in the years 1975–85, starting in Southern Europe and

Latin America. It then advanced at a prodigious rate in 1985–95, a period that saw the fall of communism in the Soviet bloc and of the apartheid regime in South Africa. Democracy's progress then began to slow, and only modest gains were achieved in the following decade, with scores peaking sometime in the early 2000s. Since then, the pattern has been one of stasis or very minor decline—certainly nothing like the "reverse waves" that Huntington identified in previous eras. The absence of democratic progress can be characterized negatively as "stagnation" or more hopefully as the conserving of prior democratic gains. But even if one discerns in the data a slight fall in the number of democracies, this cannot account for the perception of decline that has been spreading among democracy's friends and foes alike.

In my view, we must look elsewhere for the real sources of "declinist" sentiment about democracy, and several of the essays in this book can help us to locate them. A number of these sources are introduced in the latter part of Larry Diamond's chapter. One, which Diamond labels "bad governance," is elaborated in the essay by Francis Fukuyama. This term refers in the first instance to the failure of many new democracies to build effective modern states. Because of this failure, which can lead to lagging economic growth, poor public services, lack of personal security, and pervasive corruption, the citizens of such countries understandably feel disappointed by democracy. Fukuyama contends that "the legitimacy of many democracies around the world depends less on the deepening of their democratic institutions than on their ability to provide high-quality governance." Of course, bad governance afflicts most (though not all) nondemocratic countries as well, but this offers scant consolation to citizens who feel that their (democratic) government is failing them.

Fukuyama concludes that those who wish to strengthen democracy need to pay greater attention to state-building, including such prosaic matters as public administration and policy implementation. This is no doubt useful advice. Yet good governance remains stubbornly hard to achieve, especially in new democracies. In such settings, where citizens are still new to democratic attitudes and institutions, there is an almost inevitable tendency to blame poor governance on democracy. This accounts, at least in part, for democracy's tendency to break down in countries that have adopted it for the first time and its failure to take root in some places until it has been tried several times. Yet this pattern need not portend democratic failure in the long term. Many more years might be needed to attain democratic consolidation, but time would still be on the side of democracy.

THREE SOURCES OF DOUBT ABOUT DEMOCRACY

This optimistic long-term scenario, however, presupposes that democracy will remain the goal that countries are seeking. And this in turn is likely to depend on its being viewed both as the global standard of political legitimacy and as the best system for achieving the kind of prosperity and effective governance that almost all countries seek. What has changed most dramatically in recent years is that these presuppositions are increasingly being called into question. In my view, there are three chief reasons for this shift: (1) the growing sense that the advanced democracies are in trouble in terms of their economic and political performance; (2) the new self-confidence and seeming vitality of some authoritarian countries; and (3) the shifting geopolitical balance between the democracies and their rivals.

The first of these was generated by the 2008 financial crisis and its lingering economic consequences, including the recession and high unemployment rates that still plague much of Europe. That the advanced democracies suffered these reverses at a time when emerging-market countries were growing at a rapid clip undercut the notion that the institutions and policies of the West were worthy of emulation by "the rest." The political dysfunction that afflicted the advanced democracies as they sought to respond to the crisis further weakened their appeal. As Thomas Carothers notes in his essay on the changing global context of democracy promotion, "Democracy's travails in both the United States and Europe have greatly damaged the standing of democracy in the eyes of many people around the world."

The flip side of democracy's dwindling prestige has been the growing clout of a number of leading authoritarian regimes. Key among them is China, whose ability to make enormous economic strides without introducing democratic reforms has cast doubt on the notion that democracy is the only appropriate political system for wealthy countries. At the same time, China has provided developing countries with alternative sources of trade, investment, and military and development aid—with none of it tied to considerations of human rights or government accountability in the recipient states. Nor is China the only increasingly assertive nondemocratic power. Russia, Iran, Saudi Arabia, and Venezuela also have been learning from one another and even cooperating directly to thwart democracy's progress.

The *Journal*'s twenty-fifth anniversary issue also contained an article on China by Andrew J. Nathan, the first in a series that the *Journal of Democracy* will be publishing in 2015 on what we have labeled the "authoritarian resurgence." It hurts to use this title; our first *Journal of Democracy* book, published in 1993, was called *The Global Resurgence of Democracy*. But today it does seem to be authoritarianism that has the wind at its back, even if it has not yet spread to many more countries. One sign of this is the headway that the authoritarians have made in the realm of "soft power," especially in major regional and multilateral organizations. The prodemocratic norms that the democracies helped to embed in organizations such as the OSCE, the Council of Europe, and the OAS in the 1990s are being weakened by antidemocratic countries represented in these bodies. Authoritarian powers such as Russia and China also are ramping up their cultural diplomacy and international broadcasting while Western efforts in these fields have been unfocused and underfunded.

But it is not only in "soft-power" competition that the advanced democracies have fallen short. Increasingly, they are looking weaker in terms of hard power as well, shrinking their defense budgets even as authoritarian states spend more on arms. The *Journal of Democracy* has devoted little attention to issues of interstate relations or military affairs. In part, this reflected our sense of where the *Journal* enjoys a comparative advantage among world-affairs periodicals—most of them focus on security and foreign policy, while few study the domestic politics of non-Western countries. But we also felt that the internal developments accompanying or preceding struggles over democracy often were decisive in shaping the direction of international relations. Certainly that seemed true during the height of the third wave. Though the international context mattered, of course, the spark for change frequently came from internal grievances, movements, and conflicts, and by concentrating on these the *Journal* was, in our view, generally "ahead of the curve" in providing insight into how international developments would unfold.

We believe that the focus we have chosen is still the right one for the *Journal*, but I have begun to wonder whether the period of the 1990s was atypical. Perhaps this "unipolar moment" of overwhelming dominance by the United States and its democratic allies had made it possible for internal prodemocratic struggles to take center stage, creating a favorable international environment for democracy without which democracy would not have prospered. This is certainly the interpretation suggested in the chapter by Robert Kagan. As he puts it, "Geopolitical shifts among the reigning great powers, often but not always the result of wars, can have a significant effect on the domestic politics of the smaller and weaker nations of the world." Kagan asserts that the United States is in "a state of retrenchment" in the international arena and that this is inflicting "collateral damage" on the fortunes of democracy.

In 2014, these trends became manifest. The rise of the so-called Islamic State in Syria and Iraq, amid the disappointed hopes of the "Arab Spring" (outside Tunisia) and worries about Afghanistan, made it clear that Western efforts to impose some kind of order and to encourage democracy in the broader Middle East were not succeeding. Meanwhile, China's muscle-flexing in the East and South China Seas seemed to foreshadow a return to the use of force in Asia. And most important of all, Russia's brazen annexation of Crimea and stealth invasion of eastern Ukraine showed that the rules-based international order built by democratic powers could no longer be taken for granted.

If the liberal world order is indeed coming apart under pressure from the authoritarians, the future of democracy will be deeply affected. In a globe divided into spheres of influence and power blocs, a country's ability to follow a democratic path will be determined above all by its international alliances and its geography. We see a foreshadowing of this in the current struggle in Ukraine, where the country's internal efforts to build a well-functioning and stable democracy—a task that is difficult enough—are constantly challenged and sometimes overwhelmed by military and economic pressure from Russia.

This new salience of geopolitics threatens to change the rules of the game. It may both limit the centrality of the internal balance of forces in shaping a country's regime choices and increase the chances that the imposition of external force will be decisive. Moreover, if the geopolitical balance appears to be tilting the authoritarians' way, they will seem much more attractive to the many individuals and nations that seek above all to be on the stronger side. Under these conditions, democracy would lose much of its luster. Where it broke down, there would be less demand to restore it. One could no longer be confident that time would still be on democracy's side.

This gloomy scenario is far from being foreordained. The authoritarians have many weaknesses (which will grow if the recent oil-price drop persists), and democracy has many strengths, including the capacity for self-correction. Though it is often complacent and slow to move, democracy also has shown a remarkable ability to respond to crises. It was arguably in deeper trouble in the 1970s than it is today, but it bounced back. It can do so again. But first its supporters must undertake a clear-eyed appraisal of its current decline and summon the resolve and seriousness of purpose needed to reverse it.

1

Why Is Democracy Performing So Poorly?

FRANCIS FUKUYAMA

The *Journal of Democracy* published its inaugural issue a bit past the midpoint of what Samuel P. Huntington labeled the "third wave" of democratization, right after the fall of the Berlin Wall and just before the breakup of the former Soviet Union.[1] The transitions in Southern Europe and most of those in Latin America had already happened, and Eastern Europe was moving at dizzying speed away from communism, while the democratic transitions in sub-Saharan Africa and the former USSR were just getting under way. Overall, there has been remarkable worldwide progress in democratization over a period of almost 45 years, raising the number of electoral democracies from about 35 in 1970 to well over 110 in 2014.

But as Larry Diamond has pointed out, there has been a democratic recession since 2006, with a decline in aggregate Freedom House scores every year since then.[2] The year 2014 has not been good for democracy, with two big authoritarian powers, Russia and China, on the move at either end of Eurasia. The Arab Spring of

2011, which raised expectations that the Arab exception to the third wave might end, has degenerated into renewed dictatorship in the case of Egypt, and into anarchy in Libya, Yemen, and also Syria, which along with Iraq has seen the emergence of a new radical Islamist movement, the Islamic State in Iraq and Syria (ISIS).

It is hard to know whether we are experiencing a momentary setback in a general movement toward greater democracy around the world, similar to a stock-market correction, or whether the events of this year signal a broader shift in world politics and the rise of serious alternatives to democracy. In either case, it is hard not to feel that the performance of democracies around the world has been deficient in recent years. This begins with the most developed and successful democracies, those of the United States and the European Union, which experienced massive economic crises in the late 2000s and seem to be mired in a period of slow growth and stagnating incomes. But a number of newer democracies, from Brazil to Turkey to India, have also been disappointing in their performance in many respects, and subject to their own protest movements.

Spontaneous democratic movements against authoritarian regimes continue to arise out of civil society, from Ukraine and Georgia to Tunisia and Egypt to Hong Kong. But few of these movements have been successful in leading to the establishment of stable, well-functioning democracies. It is worth asking why the performance of democracy around the world has been so disappointing.

In my view, a single important factor lies at the core of many democratic setbacks over the past generation. It has to do with a failure of institutionalization—the fact that state capacity in many new and existing democracies has not kept pace with popular demands for democratic accountability. It is much harder to move from a patrimonial or neopatrimonial state to a modern, impersonal one than it is to move from an authoritarian regime to one that holds regular, free, and fair elections. It is the failure to establish modern, well-governed states that has been the Achilles heel of recent democratic transitions.

SOME DEFINITIONS

Modern liberal democracies combine three basic institutions: the state, the rule of law, and democratic accountability.

The first of these, the state, is a legitimate monopoly of coercive power that exercises its authority over a defined territory. States concentrate and employ power to keep the peace, defend communities from external enemies, enforce laws, and provide basic public goods.

The rule of law is a set of rules, reflecting community values, that are binding not just on citizens, but also on the elites who wield coercive power. If law does not constrain the powerful, it amounts to commands of the executive and constitutes merely rule *by* law.

Finally, democratic accountability seeks to ensure that government acts in the interests of the whole community, rather than simply in the self-interest of the rulers. It is usually achieved through procedures such as free and fair multiparty elections, though procedural accountability is not always coincident with substantive accountability.

A liberal democracy balances these potentially contradictory institutions. The state generates and employs power, while rule of law and democratic accountability seek to constrain power and ensure that it is used in the public interest. A state without constraining institutions is a dictatorship; a polity that is all constraint and no power is anarchic.

As Samuel Huntington used to argue, before a polity can constrain power, it must be able to employ it. In the words of Alexander Hamilton, "A feeble execution is but another phrase for a bad execution; and a government ill executed, whatever it may be in theory, must be, in practice, a bad government."[3]

There is a further critical distinction to be made between patrimonial and modern states. A modern state aspires to be *impersonal,* treating people equally on the basis of citizenship rather than on whether they have a personal relationship to the ruler. By contrast, patrimonial states are ones in which the polity is regarded as a species of personal property and in which there is no distinction between the public interest and the ruler's private interest. Today there are no fully patrimonial societies, since no one dares any longer to claim ownership of an entire country, as kings and queens did in ages past. There are, however, many neopatrimonial states that pretend to be modern polities, but these in fact constitute rent-sharing kleptocracies run for the private benefit of the insiders. Neopatrimonialism can coexist with democracy, producing widespread patronage and clientelism in which politicians share state resources with networks of political supporters. In such societies, individuals go into politics not to pursue a vision of public good, but rather to enrich themselves.

Coercion remains central to the functioning of the state, which is why state power so often generates fear and hatred. Michael Mann has famously distinguished between "despotic" and "infrastructural" power, the former related to coercion and the latter to the ability to provide public goods and look after the public interest.[4] This distinction might tempt us to say that "good" states have infrastructural power, while "bad" states make use of despotic power. But, in fact, coercion is important to all states. Successful states convert power into authority—that is, into voluntary compliance by citizens based on the belief that the state's actions are legitimate. But not all citizens agree to obey the law, and even the most legitimate democracies require police power to enforce the law. It is impossible to control corruption, for example, or to collect taxes if nobody goes to jail for violating the law. Enforcement capacity does not emerge simply through passing laws; it also requires investment in manpower and training and in establishing the institutional rules that govern its exercise.

If there is anything that the experience of the past 25 years should have taught us, it is that the democratic leg of this tripod is much easier to construct than the rule of law or the modern state. Or to put it slightly differently, the development of modern states has not kept pace with the development of democratic institutions, leading to unbalanced situations in which new (and sometimes even well-established) democracies have not been able to keep up with their citizens' demand for high-quality government services. This has led, in turn, to the delegitimation of democracy as such. Conversely, the ability of authoritarian states like China and Singapore to provide such services has increased their prestige relative to that of democracy in many parts of the world.

The recent experiences of Afghanistan and Iraq illustrate this problem. After the US invasion and occupation of these countries in 2001 and 2003, respectively, the United States was able, with some international help, to organize democratic elections that led to the seating of new governments in both countries. The quality of democracy in both places—especially in Afghanistan, where the presidential elections of 2009 and 2014 were marred by serious allegations of fraud[5]—was questioned by many, but at least a democratic process was in place to provide leadership that had some semblance of legitimacy.

What did not occur in either place was the development of a modern state that could defend the country's territory from internal and external enemies and deliver public services in a fair and impartial manner. Both countries were beset by internal insurgencies, and in 2014 the US-trained Iraqi army collapsed in the north under the onslaught of ISIS. Both countries were plagued by extremely high levels of corruption, which in turn undermined their ability to deliver government services and undercut their legitimacy. The huge investments in state-building in both places by the United States and its coalition partners seem to have had limited effect.

State-building failures also played a key role in events in Ukraine. Western friends of democracy cheered when the Orange Revolution forced a new presidential election in 2004, leading to the defeat of incumbent prime minister Viktor Yanukovych by Viktor Yushchenko. But the new Orange Coalition proved feckless and corrupt, and did nothing to improve the overall quality of governance in Ukraine. As a result, Yanukovych defeated Yushchenko in

2010 in what most observers credited as a free and fair election. Yanukovych's presidency was marked by even higher levels of predatory behavior, generating a new round of protests in Kyiv after his announcement in late 2013 that he would pursue association with Vladimir Putin's Eurasian Union rather than with the European Union. In the meantime, Putin had consolidated his increasingly illiberal rule in Russia and strengthened his state's position vis-à-vis the outside world, making possible the outright annexation of Crimea following Yanukovych's ouster in February 2014.

I would argue that the current conflict pitting Russia against the new Ukrainian government and its Western backers is less one over democracy per se than over modern versus neopatrimonial political orders. There is little question that, in the wake of the Crimean annexation, Vladimir Putin has become very popular in Russia and would be likely to win overwhelmingly if a new election were to be held. The real choice facing people in this region is a different one—whether their societies are to be based on governments seeking to serve the public interest in an impersonal manner, or are to be ruled by a corrupt coalition of elites who seek to use the state as a route to personal enrichment.

The legitimacy of many democracies around the world depends less on the deepening of their democratic institutions than on their ability to provide high-quality governance. The new Ukrainian state will not survive if it does not address the problem of pervasive corruption that brought down its Orange Coalition predecessor. Democracy has become deeply entrenched in most of Latin America over the past generation; what is lacking now in countries such as Brazil, Colombia, and Mexico is the capacity to deliver basic public goods like education, infrastructure, and citizen security. The same can be said of the world's largest democracy, India, which suffers from pervasive clientelism and corruption. In 2014, it decisively turned to the BJP's Narendra Modi in hopes that he would provide decisive leadership and strong government in place of the feckless and corrupt Congress-led coalition that had been in power for the past decade.

HOW TO GET TO A MODERN STATE

There is by now a huge literature on democratic transitions, much of it published originally in the *Journal of Democracy*. There is a much smaller literature available on the question of how to make the transition from a neopatrimonial to a modern state, though some progress has been made over the past decade and a half. This reflects a conceptual deficit, rooted in misconceptions of the nature of the underlying problem.

For example, there is a tendency to associate state modernity with the absence of corruption. Corruption, of course, is a huge problem in many societies and has generated its own large literature. But while there is a high degree of correlation between levels of corruption and poor state performance, they are not the same thing. A state may be relatively uncorrupt and yet be incapable of delivering basic services due to a lack of capacity. No one has argued, for example, that Guinea, Sierra Leone, or Liberia has been unable to deal with the recent Ebola epidemic because of pervasive corruption in their respective public-health systems; rather, the problem is one of insufficient human and material resources—doctors, nurses, and hospitals with electricity, clean water, and the like.

"State capacity" therefore comes much closer than the absence of corruption to describing what is at the core of state modernity. Modern states provide a bewildering array of complex services, from keeping economic and social statistics to providing disaster relief, forecasting the weather, and controlling the flight paths of airplanes. All these activities require huge investments in human resources and in the material conditions that allow agents of the state to operate; the simple absence of corruption does not mean that these will exist. Yet even the term "state capacity" fails to capture the ends that this capacity serves and the degree to which it is being employed impersonally.

There is, moreover, a serious lack of clarity about the ways in which strong state capacity has been generated in the past. At the moment, there is something of a consensus within the international donor community on how to pursue good governance, a consensus that is embedded in programs like participatory budgeting, the Open Government Partnership, and the initiatives of the numerous organizations promoting government transparency around the world. Underlying these approaches is the theory that good governance is the product of greater transparency and accountability. These approaches assume that more information about government corruption or malfeasance will lead to citizen anger and demands for better state performance, which will in turn push governments to reform themselves. Better-quality democracy, in other words, is seen as the solution to the problem of corruption and weak state capacity.

The only problem with this strategy is that there is strikingly little empirical evidence demonstrating that such an approach is how existing high-performing governments have been created, either historically or under contemporary circumstances. Many states with relatively high-performing governments—China, Japan, Germany, France, and Denmark, for example—created modern "Weberian" bureaucracies under authoritarian conditions; those that subsequently went on to become democracies inherited meritocratic state apparatuses that simply survived the transition. The motive for creating modern governments was not grassroots pressure from informed and mobilized citizens but rather elite pressure, often for reasons of national security. Charles Tilly's famous aphorism that "war makes the state and the state makes war" sums up the experience not just of much of early modern Europe but also of China during the Spring and Autumn and Warring States periods, leading to the emergence of an impersonal state during the Qin unification in the third century BCE.[6]

Similarly, there is strikingly little evidence that current donor and NGO efforts to promote good governance through increasing transparency and accountability have had a measurable impact on state performance.[7] The theory that there should be a correlation between the increased availability of information about government performance and the quality of final government outputs rests on a number of heroic assumptions—that citizens will care about poor government performance (as opposed to being content to benefit from practices like ethnic-based patronage); that they are capable of organizing politically to put pressure on the government; that the country's political institutions are ones that accurately transmit grassroots sentiment to politicians in ways that make the latter accountable; and finally, that the government actually has the capacity to perform as citizens demand.

The actual history of the relationship between state modernity and democracy is far more complicated than the contemporary theory suggests. Following the framework first established by Martin Shefter, I have argued elsewhere that the sequence by which democracy (measured by the degree of universality of the franchise) and state modernity were established has determined the long-term quality of government.[8] Where a modern state has been consolidated before the extension of the franchise, it has often succeeded in surviving into modern times; where the democratic opening preceded state reform, the result has often been widespread clientelism. This was true above all in the country that first opened the franchise to all white males, the United States, which went on to create the world's first pervasively clientelistic political system (known in US history as the spoils, or patronage, system). In that country during the nineteenth century, democracy and state quality were clearly at odds with each other. The reason for this is that, in democracies with low levels of income and education, individualized voter incentives (the essence of clientelism) are more likely to mobilize voters and get them to the polls than are promises of programmatic public policies.[9]

The situation changes, however, at higher levels of economic development. Higher-income voters are harder to bribe through an individualized payment, and they tend to care more about programmatic policies. In addition, higher levels of development are usually driven by the growth of a market economy, which provides alternative avenues for personal enrichment outside of politics. The last Taiwanese election during which clientelism was widespread occurred in the early 1990s; thereafter, Taiwanese voters were too wealthy to be easily bribable.[10]

Although democracy is a driver of clientelism at low levels of per capita income, it may open a path toward the creation of higher-quality government as nations grow richer. The United States is again an example: By the 1880s, the country was rapidly transforming itself from an agrarian society into an urban industrial one, knitted together in a gigantic continental market by new technologies like railroads. Economic growth drove the emergence of new economic actors—urban professionals, a more complex set of business interests, and middle-class individuals more generally—who wanted higher-quality government and had no strong stake in the existing patronage system. A grassroots movement made possible the 1883 passage of the Pendleton Act, which established the principle of merit-based recruitment into the federal bureaucracy that presidents Theodore Roosevelt (1901–09) and Woodrow Wilson (1913–21) would do much to promote. Party bosses and political machines continued to thrive for several generations past that point, but they were gradually eliminated in most US cities by the middle of the twentieth century through determined political campaigning. If contemporary democracies like India and Brazil are to deal with problems of patronage and corruption, they will have to follow a similar route.

THE NECESSITY OF ENFORCEMENT

The United States had one important advantage, however, that is lacking in many of today's new democracies. It always had strong police power and could enforce the laws that it passed. This capacity was rooted in the Common Law, which the colonies inherited from England and had become well-institutionalized before their independence. American governments at all levels always maintained relatively strong police power to indict, try, and convict criminals at various levels of government. This coercive power was backed by a strong belief in the legitimacy of law and was therefore converted into genuine authority in most places. The capacity to enforce constitutes an area where state capacity overlaps with the rule of law, and it is critical in dealing with a problem like corruption. The behavior of public officials depends on incentives—not just getting adequate pay for doing their jobs, but the fear of punishment if they break the law. In very many countries, taxes are not paid and bribes are collected because there is very little likelihood of lawbreakers going to jail.

Effective enforcement was central to the success of one of the most notable recent efforts to improve public-sector performance, that of Georgia. Following the 2003 Rose Revolution, the government of Mikheil Saakashvili cracked down on corruption on a number of fronts, tackling the traffic police, tax evasion, and the pervasive operations of criminal gangs known as the "thieves-in-law." While some of this was done through transparency initiatives and positive incentives (e.g., by publishing government data online and by increasing police salaries by an order of magnitude), effective enforcement was dependent on the creation of new police units that did things like making highly publicized arrests of high-ranking former officials and businessmen. By the end of the Saakashvili administration, this enhanced police power had come to be abused in many ways, setting off a political reaction that led to the election of Bidzina Ivanishvili and the Georgian Dream party.[11]

Such abuses should not obscure the importance of the state's coercive power in achieving effective enforcement of the law. Controlling corruption requires the wholesale shifting of a population's normative expectations of behavior—if everyone around me is taking bribes, I will look like a fool if I do not participate as well. Under these circumstances, fear is a much more effective motivator than good intentions or economic incentives. Prior to the Rose Revolution, Georgia had the reputation of being one of the most corrupt places in the former Soviet Union. Today, by a number of governance measures, it has become one of the least corrupt. It is hard to find examples of effectively governed polities that do not exert substantial coercive power. Contemporary efforts to promote good governance through increased transparency and accountability without simultaneously incorporating efforts to strengthen enforcement power are doomed to fail in the end.

In *Political Order in Changing Societies,* Samuel Huntington argued that the political dimensions of development often fail to keep pace with social mobilization and thus lead to political disorder. There can be a corresponding failure of state institutions to keep up with the development of democratic ones.

This conclusion has a number of important implications for the way in which the United States and other democracies pursue democracy promotion. In the past, there has been heavy emphasis on leveling the playing field in authoritarian countries through support for civil society organizations, and on supporting the initial transition away from dictatorship.

Creating a viable democracy, however, requires two further stages during which the initial mobilization against tyranny gets institutionalized and converted into durable practices. The first is the organization of social movements into political parties that can contest elections. Civil society organizations usually focus on narrow issues, and are not set up to mobilize voters—this is the unique domain of political parties. The failure to build political parties explains why more liberal forces have frequently failed at the ballot box in transitional countries from Russia to Ukraine to Egypt.

The second required stage, however, concerns state-building and state capacity. Once a democratic government is in power, it must actually *govern*—that is, it must exercise legitimate authority and provide basic services to the population. The democracy-promotion community has paid much less attention to the problems of democratic governance than it has to the initial mobilization and the transition. Without the ability to govern well, however, new democracies will disappoint the expectations of their followers and delegitimate themselves. Indeed, as US history shows, democratization without attention to state modernization can actually lead to a weakening of the quality of government.

This does not mean, however, that state modernization can

be achieved only under conditions of authoritarian rule. The fact that many long-established democracies followed the sequence of state-building prior to democratization—what Samuel Huntington labeled the "authoritarian transition"—does not necessarily mean that this is a viable strategy for countries in the contemporary world, where popular demands and expectations for democracy are so much higher.

For better or worse, many countries around the world will have to develop modern states at the same time that they build democratic institutions and the rule of law. This means that the democracy-promotion community needs to pay much more attention to the building of modern states, and not relax when authoritarian governments are pushed out of power. This also suggests an expanded intellectual agenda for the *Journal of Democracy*: Along with its substantial contributions to the study of how democracies emerge and become consolidated, it needs to focus renewed attention on how modern state institutions come into being and fall into decay.

NOTES

1. Samuel P. Huntington, *The Third Wave: Democratization in the Late Twentieth Century* (Oklahoma City: University of Oklahoma Press, 1991).
2. See Larry Diamond's chapter, "Facing Up to the Democratic Recession," in this volume.
3. Alexander Hamilton, *Federalist* 70 (1788).
4. Michael Mann, *The Sources of Social Power,* vol. 1, *A History of Power from the Beginning to AD 1760* (Cambridge: Cambridge University Press, 1986).
5. See Sarah Chayes, *Thieves of State: Why Corruption Threatens Global Security* (New York: W. W. Norton, 2015).
6. This point is made in my book *The Origins of Political Order: From Prehuman Times to the French Revolution* (New York: Farrar, Straus & Giroux, 2011).
7. See, for example, Ivar Kolstad and Arne Wiig, "Is Transparency the Key to Reducing Corruption in Resource-Rich Countries?" *World Development* 37 (March 2009): 521–32; Mehmet Bac, "Corruption, Connections

and Transparency: Does a Better Screen Imply a Better Scene?" *Public Choice* 107 (April 2001): 87–96; Susan Rose-Ackerman and Rory Truex, "Corruption and Policy Reform," working paper prepared for the Copenhagen Consensus Project, 27 February 2012; and Luca Etter, "Can Transparency Reduce Corruption?" paper presented at the Doing Business Conference, Georgetown University, Washington, DC, February 2014.

8. See Martin Shefter, *Political Parties and the State: The American Historical Experience* (Princeton: Princeton University Press, 1994).
9. See Francis Fukuyama, "Democracy and the Quality of the State," *Journal of Democracy* 24 (October 2013): 5–16.
10. Mushtaq H. Khan, "Markets, States, and Democracy: Patron-Client Networks and the Case for Democracy in Developing Countries," *Democratization* 12 (December 2005): 704–24; Chin-Shou Wang and Charles Kurzman, "The Logistics: How to Buy Votes," in Frederic Charles Schaffer, ed., *Elections for Sale: The Causes and Consequences of Vote Buying* (Boulder, CO: Lynne Rienner, 2007).
11. See World Bank, *Fighting Corruption in Public Services: Chronicling Georgia's Reforms* (Washington, DC: World Bank, 2012); Peter Pomerantsev et al., "Revolutionary Tactics: Insights from Police and Justice Reform in Georgia," Legatum Institute, London, June 2014.

2

The Weight of Geopolitics

ROBERT KAGAN

Politics follows geopolitics, or so it has often seemed throughout history. When the Athenian democracy's empire rose in the fifth century BCE, the number of Greek city-states ruled by democrats proliferated; Sparta's power was reflected in the spread of Spartan-style oligarchies. When the Soviet Union's power rose in the early Cold War years, communism spread. In the later Cold War years, when the United States and Western Europe gained the advantage and ultimately triumphed, democracies proliferated and communism collapsed. Was this all just the outcome of the battle of ideas, as Francis Fukuyama and others argue, with the better idea of liberal capitalism triumphing over the worse ideas of communism and fascism? Or did liberal ideas triumph in part because of real battles and shifts that occurred less in the realm of thought than in the realm of power?

These are relevant questions again. We live in a time when democratic nations are in retreat in the realm of geopolitics, and when democracy itself is also in retreat. The latter phenomenon has been well documented by Freedom House, which has recorded declines in freedom in the world for nine straight years. At the level of geopolitics, the shifting tectonic plates have yet to produce a seismic rearrangement of power, but rumblings are audible. The United States has been in a state of retrenchment since President Barack Obama took office in 2009. The democratic nations of Europe, which some might have expected to pick up the slack, have instead turned inward and all but abandoned earlier dreams of reshaping the international system in their image. As for such rising democracies as Brazil, India, Turkey, and South Africa, they are neither rising as fast as once anticipated nor yet behaving as democracies in world affairs. Their focus remains narrow and regional. Their national identities remain shaped by postcolonial and nonaligned sensibilities—by old but carefully nursed resentments—which lead them, for instance, to shield rather than condemn autocratic Russia's invasion of democratic Ukraine or, in the case of Brazil, to prefer the company of Venezuelan dictators to that of North American democratic presidents.

Meanwhile, insofar as there is energy in the international system, it comes from the great-power autocracies, China and Russia, and from would-be theocrats pursuing their dream of a new caliphate in the Middle East. For all their many problems and weaknesses, it is still these autocracies and these aspiring religious totalitarians that push forward while the democracies draw back, that act while the democracies react, and that seem increasingly unleashed while the democracies feel increasingly constrained.

It should not be surprising that one of the side effects of these circumstances has been the weakening and in some cases collapse of democracy in those places where it was newest and weakest. Geopolitical shifts among the reigning great powers, often but not always the result of wars, can have significant effects on the domestic politics of the smaller and weaker nations of the world. Global democratizing trends have been stopped and reversed before.

Consider the interwar years. In 1920, when the number of democracies in the world had doubled in the aftermath of the First

World War, contemporaries such as the British historian James Bryce believed that they were witnessing "a natural trend, due to a general law of social progress."[1] Yet almost immediately the new democracies in Estonia, Latvia, Lithuania, and Poland began to fall. Europe's democratic great powers, France and Britain, were suffering the effects of the recent devastating war, while the one rich and healthy democratic power, the United States, had retreated to the safety of its distant shores. In the vacuum came Mussolini's rise to power in Italy in 1922, the crumbling of Germany's Weimar Republic, and the broader triumph of European fascism. Greek democracy fell in 1936. Spanish democracy fell to Franco that same year. Military coups overthrew democratic governments in Portugal, Brazil, Uruguay, and Argentina. Japan's shaky democracy succumbed to military rule and then to a form of fascism.

Across three continents, fragile democracies gave way to authoritarian forces exploiting the vulnerabilities of the democratic system, while other democracies fell prey to the worldwide economic depression. There was a ripple effect, too—the success of fascism in one country strengthened similar movements elsewhere, sometimes directly. Spanish fascists received military assistance from the fascist regimes in Germany and Italy. The result was that by 1939 the democratic gains of the previous 40 years had been wiped out.

The period after the First World War showed not only that democratic gains could be reversed but also that democracy need not always triumph even in the competition of ideas. For it was not just that democracies had been overthrown; the very idea of democracy had been "discredited," as John A. Hobson observed.[2] Democracy's aura of inevitability vanished as great numbers of people rejected the idea that it was a better form of government. Human beings, after all, do not yearn only for freedom, autonomy, individuality, and recognition. Especially in times of difficulty, they yearn also for comfort, security, order, and, importantly, a sense of belonging to something larger than themselves, something that submerges autonomy and individuality—all of which autocracies can sometimes provide, or at least appear to provide, better than democracies.

In the 1920s and 1930s, the fascist governments looked stronger, more energetic and efficient, and more capable of providing reassurance in troubled times. They appealed effectively to nationalist, ethnic, and tribal sentiments. The many weaknesses of Germany's Weimar democracy, inadequately supported by the democratic great powers, and of the fragile and short-lived democracies of Italy and Spain made their people susceptible to the appeals of the Nazis, Mussolini, and Franco, just as the weaknesses of Russian democracy in the 1990s made a more authoritarian government under Vladimir Putin attractive to many Russians. People tend to follow winners, and between the wars the democratic-capitalist countries looked weak and in retreat compared with the apparently vigorous fascist regimes and with Stalin's Soviet Union.

It took a second world war and another military victory by the Allied democracies (plus the Soviet Union) to reverse the trend again. The United States imposed democracy by force and through prolonged occupations in West Germany, Italy, Japan, Austria, and South Korea. With the victory of the democracies and the discrediting of fascism—chiefly on the battlefield—many other countries followed suit. Greece and Turkey both moved in a democratic direction, as did Brazil, Argentina, Peru, Ecuador, Venezuela, and Colombia. Some of the new nations born as Europe shed its colonies also experimented with democratic government, the most prominent example being India. By 1950, the number of democracies had grown to between twenty and thirty, and they governed close to 40 percent of the world's population.

Was this the victory of an idea or the victory of arms? Was it the product of an inevitable human evolution or, as Samuel P. Huntington later observed, of "historically discrete events"?[3] We would prefer to believe the former, but evidence suggests the latter, for it turned out that even the great wave of democracy following World War II was not irreversible. Another "reverse wave" hit from the late 1950s through the early 1970s. Peru, Brazil, Argentina, Bolivia, Chile, Uruguay, Ecuador, South Korea, the Philippines, Pakistan, Indonesia, and Greece all fell back under authoritarian rule. In Africa,

Nigeria was the most prominent of the newly decolonized nations where democracy failed. By 1975, more than three dozen governments around the world had been installed by military coups.[4] Few spoke of democracy's inevitability in the 1970s or even in the early 1980s. As late as 1984, Huntington himself believed that "the limits of democratic development in the world" had been reached, noting the "unreceptivity to democracy of several major cultural traditions," as well as "the substantial power of antidemocratic governments (particularly the Soviet Union)."[5]

But then, unexpectedly, came the "third wave." From the mid-1970s through the early 1990s, the number of democracies in the world rose to an astonishing 120, representing well over half the world's population. What explained the prolonged success of democratization over the last quarter of the twentieth century? It could not have been merely the steady rise of the global economy and the general yearning for freedom, autonomy, and recognition. Neither economic growth nor human yearnings had prevented the democratic reversals of the 1960s and early 1970s. Until the third wave, many nations around the world careened back and forth between democracy and authoritarianism in a cyclical, almost predictable manner. What was most notable about the third wave was that this cyclical alternation between democracy and autocracy was interrupted. Nations moved into a democratic phase and stayed there. But why?

THE INTERNATIONAL CLIMATE IMPROVES

The answer is related to the configuration of power and ideas in the world. The international climate from the mid-1970s onward was simply more hospitable to democracies and more challenging to autocratic governments than had been the case in past eras. In his study, Huntington emphasized the change, following the Second Vatican Council, in the Catholic Church's doctrine regarding order and revolution, which tended to weaken the legitimacy of authoritarian governments in Catholic countries. The growing success and attractiveness of the European Community (EC), meanwhile, had an impact on the internal policies of nations such as Portugal, Greece, and Spain, which sought the economic benefits of membership in the EC and therefore felt pressure to conform to its democratic norms. These norms increasingly became international norms. But they did not appear out of nowhere or as the result of some natural evolution of the human species. As Huntington noted, "The pervasiveness of democratic norms rested in large part on the commitment to those norms of the most powerful country in the world."[6]

The United States, in fact, played a critical role in making the explosion of democracy possible. This was not because US policy makers consistently promoted democracy around the world. They did not. At various times throughout the Cold War, US policy often supported dictatorships as part of the battle against communism or simply out of indifference. It even permitted or was complicit in the overthrow of democratic regimes deemed unreliable—those of Mohammad Mossadegh in Iran in 1953, Jacobo Arbenz in Guatemala in 1954, and Salvador Allende in Chile in 1973. At times, US foreign policy was almost hostile to democracy. President Richard Nixon regarded it as "not necessarily the best form of government for people in Asia, Africa, and Latin America."[7]

Nor, when the United States did support democracy, was it purely out of fealty to principle. Often it was for strategic reasons. Officials in President Ronald Reagan's administration came to believe that democratic governments might actually be *better* than autocracies at fending off communist insurgencies, for instance. And often it was popular local demands that compelled the United States to make a choice that it would otherwise have preferred to avoid, between supporting an unpopular and possibly faltering dictatorship and "getting on the side of the people." Reagan would have preferred to support the dictatorship of Ferdinand Marcos in the 1980s had he not been confronted by the moral challenge of Filipino "people power." Rarely if ever did the United States seek a change of regime primarily out of devotion to democratic principles.

Beginning in the mid-1970s, however, the general inclination of the United States did begin to shift toward a more critical view of dictatorship. The US Congress, led by human-rights advocates, began to condition or cut off US aid to authoritarian allies, which weakened their hold on power. In the Helsinki Accords of 1975, a reference to human-rights issues drew greater attention to the cause of dissidents and other opponents of dictatorship in the Eastern bloc. President Jimmy Carter focused attention on the human-rights abuses of the Soviet Union as well as of right-wing governments in Latin America and elsewhere. The US government's international information services, including the Voice of America and Radio Free Europe/Radio Liberty, put greater emphasis on democracy and human rights in their programming. The Reagan administration, after first trying to roll back Carter's human-rights agenda, eventually embraced it and made the promotion of democracy part of its stated (if not always its actual) policy. Even during this period, US policy was far from consistent. Many allied dictatorships, especially in the Middle East, were not only tolerated but actively supported with US economic and military aid. But the net effect of the shift in US policy, joined with the efforts of Europe, was significant.

The third wave began in 1974 in Portugal, where the Carnation Revolution put an end to a half-century of dictatorship. As Larry Diamond notes, this revolution did not just happen. The United States and the European democracies played a key role, making a "heavy investment . . . in support of the democratic parties."[8] Over the next decade and a half, the United States used a variety of tools, including direct military intervention, to aid democratic transitions and prevent the undermining of existing fragile democracies all across the globe. In 1978, Carter threatened military action in the Dominican Republic when long-serving president Joaquín Balaguer refused to give up power after losing an election. In 1983, Reagan's invasion of Grenada restored a democratic government after a military coup. In 1986, the United States threatened military action to prevent Marcos from forcibly annulling an election that he had lost. In 1989, President George H. W. Bush invaded Panama to help install democracy after military strongman Manuel Noriega had annulled his nation's elections.

Throughout this period, too, the United States used its influence to block military coups in Honduras, Bolivia, El Salvador, Peru, and South Korea. Elsewhere it urged presidents not to try staying in office beyond constitutional limits. Huntington estimated that over the course of about a decade and a half, US support had been "critical to democratization in the Dominican Republic, Grenada, El Salvador, Guatemala, Honduras, Uruguay, Peru, Ecuador, Panama, and the Philippines" and was "a contributing factor to democratization in Portugal, Chile, Poland, Korea, Bolivia, and Taiwan."[9]

Many developments both global and local helped to produce the democratizing trend of the late 1970s and the 1980s, and there might have been a democratic wave even if the United States had not been so influential. The question is whether the wave would have been as large and as lasting. The stable zones of democracy in Europe and Japan proved to be powerful magnets. The liberal free-market and free-trade system increasingly outperformed the stagnating economies of the socialist bloc, especially at the dawn of the information revolution. The greater activism of the United States, together with that of other successful democracies, helped to build a broad, if not universal, consensus that was more sympathetic to democratic forms of government and less sympathetic to authoritarian forms.

Diamond and others have noted how important it was that these "global democratic norms" came to be "reflected in regional and international institutions and agreements as never before."[10] Those norms had an impact on the internal political processes of countries, making it harder for authoritarians to weather political and economic storms and easier for democratic movements to gain legitimacy. But "norms" are transient as well. In the 1930s, the trendsetting nations were fascist dictatorships. In the 1950s and 1960s, variants of socialism were in vogue. But from the 1970s until recently, the United States and a handful of other democratic powers set the fashion trend. They pushed—some might even say imposed—democratic principles and embedded them in international institutions and agreements.

Equally important was the role that the United States played in preventing backsliding away from democracy where it had barely taken root. Perhaps the most significant US contribution was simply to prevent military coups against fledgling democratic governments. In a sense, the United States was interfering in what might have been a natural cycle, preventing nations that ordinarily would have been "due" for an authoritarian phase from following the usual pattern. It was not that the United States was exporting democracy everywhere. More often, it played the role of "catcher in the rye"—preventing young democracies from falling off the cliff—in places such as the Philippines, Colombia, and Panama. This helped to give the third wave unprecedented breadth and durability.

Finally, there was the collapse of the Soviet Union and with it the fall of Central and Eastern Europe's communist regimes and their replacement by democracies. What role the United States played in hastening the Soviet downfall may be in dispute, but surely it played some part, both by containing the Soviet empire militarily and by outperforming it economically and technologically. And at the heart of the struggle were the peoples of the former Warsaw Pact countries themselves. They had long yearned to achieve the liberation of their respective nations from the Soviet Union, which also meant liberation from communism. These peoples wanted to join the rest of Europe, which offered an economic and social model that was even more attractive than that of the United States.

That Central and East Europeans uniformly chose democratic forms of government, however, was not simply the fruit of aspirations for freedom or comfort. It also reflected the desires of these peoples to place themselves under the US security umbrella. The strategic, the economic, the political, and the ideological were thus inseparable. Those nations that wanted to be part of NATO, and later of the European Union, knew that they would stand no chance of admission without democratic credentials. These democratic transitions, which turned the third wave into a democratic tsunami, need not have occurred had the world been configured differently. That a democratic, united, and prosperous Western Europe was even there to exert a powerful magnetic pull on its eastern neighbors was due to US actions after World War II.

THE LOST FUTURE OF 1848

Contrast the fate of democratic movements in the late twentieth century with that of the liberal revolutions that swept Europe in 1848. Beginning in France, the "Springtime of the Peoples," as it was known, included liberal reformers and constitutionalists, nationalists, and representatives of the rising middle class as well as radical workers and socialists. In a matter of weeks, they toppled kings and princes and shook thrones in France, Poland, Austria, and Romania, as well as the Italian peninsula and the German principalities. In the end, however, the liberal movements failed, partly because they lacked cohesion, but also because the autocratic powers forcibly crushed them. The Prussian army helped to defeat liberal movements in the German lands, while the Russian czar sent his troops into Romania and Hungary. Tens of thousands of protesters were killed in the streets of Europe. The sword proved mightier than the pen.

It mattered that the more liberal powers, Britain and France, adopted a neutral posture throughout the liberal ferment, even though France's own revolution had sparked and inspired the pan-European movement. The British monarchy and aristocracy were afraid of radicalism at home. Both France and Britain were more concerned with preserving peace among the great powers than with providing assistance to fellow liberals. The preservation of the European balance among the five great powers benefited the forces of counterrevolution everywhere, and the Springtime of the Peoples was suppressed.[11] As a result, for several decades the forces of reaction in Europe were strengthened against the forces of liberalism.

Scholars have speculated about how differently Europe and the world might have evolved had the liberal revolutions of 1848 succeeded: How might German history have unfolded had national unification been achieved under a liberal parliamentary system rather than under the leadership of Otto von Bismarck? The "Iron Chancellor" unified the nation not through elections and debates but through military victories won by the great power of the conservative Prussian army under the Hohenzollern dynasty. As the historian A. J. P. Taylor observed, history reached a turning point in 1848, but Germany "failed to turn."[12] Might Germans have learned a different lesson from the one that Bismarck taught—namely, that "the great questions of the age are not decided by speeches and majority decisions . . . but by blood and iron"?[13] Yet the international system of the day was not configured in such a way as to encourage liberal and democratic change. The European balance of power in the mid-nineteenth century did not favor democracy, and so it is not surprising that democracy failed to triumph anywhere.[14]

We can also speculate about how differently today's world might have evolved without the US role in shaping an international environment favorable to democracy, and how it might evolve should the United States find itself no longer strong enough to play that role. Democratic transitions are not inevitable, even where the conditions may be ripe. Nations may enter a transition zone—economically, socially, and politically—where the probability of moving in a democratic direction increases or decreases. But foreign influences, usually exerted by the reigning great powers, often determine which direction change takes. Strong authoritarian powers willing to support conservative forces against liberal movements can undo what might otherwise have been a "natural" evolution to democracy, just as powerful democratic nations can help liberal forces that, left to their own devices, might otherwise fail.

In the 1980s as in the 1840s, liberal movements arose for their own reasons in different countries, but their success or failure was influenced by the balance of power at the international level. In the era of US predominance, the balance was generally favorable to democracy, which helps to explain why the liberal revolutions of that later era succeeded. Had the United States not been so powerful, there would have been fewer transitions to democracy, and those that occurred might have been short-lived. It might have meant a shallower and more easily reversed third wave.[15]

DEMOCRACY, AUTOCRACY, AND POWER

What about today? With the democratic superpower curtailing its global influence, regional powers are setting the tone in their respective regions. Not surprisingly, dictatorships are more common in the environs of Russia, along the borders of China (North Korea, Burma, and Thailand), and in the Middle East, where long dictatorial traditions have so far mostly withstood the challenge of popular uprisings.

But even in regions where democracies remain strong, authoritarians have been able to make a determined stand while their democratic neighbors passively stand by. Thus Hungary's leaders, in the heart of an indifferent Europe, proclaim their love of illiberalism and crack down on press and political freedoms while the rest of the European Union, supposedly a club for democracies only, looks away. In South America, democracy is engaged in a contest with dictatorship, but an indifferent Brazil looks on, thinking only of trade and of North American imperialism. Meanwhile in Central America, next door to an indifferent Mexico, democracy collapses under the weight of drugs and crime and the resurgence of the *caudillos.* Yet it may be unfair to blame regional powers for not doing what they have never done. Insofar as the shift in the geopolitical equation has affected the fate of democracies worldwide, it is probably the change in the democratic superpower's behavior that bears most of the responsibility.

If that superpower does not change its course, we are likely to see democracy around the world rolled back further. There is nothing inevitable about democracy. The liberal world order we have been living in these past decades was not bequeathed by "the Laws of Nature and of Nature's God." It is not the endpoint of human progress.

There are those who would prefer a world order different from the liberal one. Until now, however, they have not been able to have their way, but not because their ideas of governance are impossible to enact. Who is to say that Putinism in Russia or China's particular brand of authoritarianism will not survive as far into the future as European democracy, which, after all, is less than a century old on most of the continent? Autocracy in Russia and China has certainly been around longer than any Western democracy. Indeed, it is autocracy, not democracy, that has been the norm in human history—only in recent decades have the democracies, led by the United States, had the power to shape the world.

Skeptics of US "democracy promotion" have long argued that many of the places where the democratic experiment has been tried over the past few decades are not a natural fit for that form of government and that the United States has tried to plant democracy in some very infertile soils. Given that democratic governments have taken deep root in widely varying circumstances, from impoverished India to "Confucian" East Asia to Islamic Indonesia, we ought to have some modesty about asserting where the soil is right or not right for democracy. Yet it should be clear that the prospects for democracy have been much better under the protection of a liberal world order, supported and defended by a democratic superpower or by a collection of democratic great powers. Today, as always, democracy is a fragile flower. It requires constant support, constant tending, and the plucking of weeds and fencing-off of the jungle that threaten it both from within and without. In the absence of such efforts, the jungle and the weeds may sooner or later come back to reclaim the land.

NOTES

1. Quoted in Samuel P. Huntington, *The Third Wave: Democratization in the Late Twentieth Century* (Norman: University of Oklahoma Press, 1991), 17.
2. Quoted in John Keane, *The Life and Death of Democracy* (New York: W. W. Norton, 2009), 573.
3. Huntington, *Third Wave,* 40.

4. Huntington, *Third Wave,* 21.
5. Samuel P. Huntington, "Will More Countries Become Democratic?" *Political Science Quarterly* 99 (Summer 1984): 193–218; quoted in Larry Diamond, *The Spirit of Democracy: The Struggle to Build Free Societies Throughout the World* (New York: Times Books, 2008), 10.
6. Huntington, *Third Wave,* 47.
7. Odd Arne Westad, *The Global Cold War: Third World Interventions and the Making of Our Times* (Cambridge: Cambridge University Press, 2005), 196.
8. Diamond, *Spirit of Democracy,* 5.
9. Huntington, *Third Wave,* 98.
10. Diamond, *Spirit of Democracy,* 13.
11. Mike Rapport, *1848: Year of Revolution* (New York: Basic Books, 2009), 409.
12. A. J. P. Taylor, *The Course of German History: A Survey of the Development of German History Since 1815* (1945; London: Routledge, 2001), 71.
13. Rapport, *1848,* 401–402.
14. As Huntington paraphrased the findings of Jonathan Sunshine: "External influences in Europe before 1830 were fundamentally antidemocratic and hence held up democratization. Between 1830 and 1930 . . . the external environment was neutral . . . hence democratization proceeded in different countries more or less at the pace set by economic and social development." Huntington, *Third Wave,* 86.
15. As Huntington observed, "The absence of the United States from the process would have meant fewer and later transitions to democracy." Huntington, *Third Wave,* 98.

3

Crisis and Transition, but Not Decline

PHILIPPE C. SCHMITTER

There seems to be an overwhelming consensus among scholars and politicians that democracy *as a practice* is in decline. An 18 August 2014 Google search for *decline of democracy* yielded more than 55.5 million results; Google Scholar, which searches only academic literature, still produced a hefty 434,000 hits. At the same time, however, it is widely accepted that the desire for democracy *as an ideal*—that is, self-rule by citizens possessing equal rights and having equal influence over the choice of leaders and the conduct of public affairs—has never been greater or more broadly distributed. This gap between what is promised and what is delivered has been an omnipresent feature of those long-established regimes that I have called "really existing democracies," and it has been reproduced in newly established democracies as well. It is the source of most of the historical struggles that have periodically led to the reform of democratic institutions.

A widening of this gap between the real and the ideal characterizes the present crisis—hence the growing pressure, not to dismantle or destroy democracy as such, but rather to change the way in which it is being practiced. No one seems to believe that either really existing democracies or newer democracies that have passed some threshold of consolidation will in the foreseeable future regress to their status quo ante. Moreover, there is simply no plausible alternative in sight, save for a few models (e.g., Chinese meritocracy, Russian neo-czarism, Arab monarchy, or Islamic theocracy) that are unlikely to appeal far beyond their borders. In other words (to paraphrase a line in Giuseppe Tomasi di Lampedusa's novel *The Leopard*), democracy will definitely survive, but only by changing. What these changes will be, however, is by no means clear.

SOME MISLEADING EVIDENCE OF DECLINE

Evidence for the recent crisis and decline of democracy rests on dubious conclusions from quantitative sources and selective inferences from qualitative case studies. Freedom House has served as the "definitive" source for the former, and its annual report has been featuring various versions of the "democracy-in-retreat" narrative since 2008. It has based this assertion on a decline in the average scores of its compound indicator. This is especially misleading since many so-called Free regimes have no room for improvement given the upper limits of the variables used. For example, none of the reform measures to be discussed below would increase the score of a single one of them. Many Not Free regimes have no further room for decline, and many of these are "failed states" that are locked into civil wars and have no regime at all. It is mostly the Partly Free or hybrid democracies that have shown variation—and some of that has been upward. Moreover, small changes in the average for the whole sample (which is what tends to be used as the indicator for decline) can be attributed to a relatively small number of cases, from Russia and its Eurasian former republics to Bangladesh,

Fiji, Guinea-Bissau, Mali, Mauritania, and Niger. One alternative quantitative source, the Economist Intelligence Unit's Index of Democracy, reports similar aggregate results, while another, the Bertelsmann Transformation Index, shows no significant overall change from 2006 to 2010.

Random public-opinion surveys in both new and established democracies routinely "discover" that a growing share of citizens feel that their votes do not count and are disregarded by their leaders. Most dramatic has been the decline in trust in core democratic institutions—namely, elected politicians, political parties, and legislatures. Yet these same surveys often reveal a similar decline in trust in nonelected authorities, including the military and the police, public administrators, and even scientists and physicians. In other words, skepticism has come to characterize public opinion in general, even if it is focused most intensely on the political process. Interestingly, these surveys also tell us that public interest in politics has been rising along with the sense that politics actually has a real impact on people's lives. So the gap does exist, but so does the awareness of it and, presumably, the desire to narrow it.

On the qualitative side, scholars have found a litany of "morbidity symptoms" that illustrate the extent of decline in many really existing and newly established democracies. At the top of the list, one usually finds increasing distrust of elected politicians and representative institutions (especially political parties), followed by declining levels of electoral participation and party membership or identification, rising electoral volatility, and problems in forming stable governments.

Previously dominant centrist parties find that their ideologies are no longer credible to the public and that they are losing votes to newly emerging populist parties of either the left or the right. Parliaments have become less central to the decision-making process, having been displaced by the concentration of executive power and a wider role for "guardian institutions" dominated by (allegedly) independent technocrats. Governing cabinets include ever more unelected members who are chosen for their "nonpartisan" status.

Membership in and conformity to class-based intermediary organizations such as trade unions and employers' associations have declined, while large firms, especially financial ones, have gained more direct access to the highest circles of decision making.

The "usual suspects" are typically cited as the generic causes of crisis and decline. At the top of the list, one almost always finds globalization, since it has supposedly deprived the nation-state of its former autonomy, undermining government effectiveness and responsiveness to citizen demands. Multinational enterprises, international financial institutions, and (at least in Europe) multilayered regional-governance arrangements have imposed a complex mixture of constraints and opportunities that greatly limit economic and social-policy agendas as well as the capacity to regulate and tax capitalists and their enterprises. Changes in the structure of production and the sectoral composition of the economy have weakened the collective consciousness of workers and blurred the class cleavage that had long provided the basis for political parties on the left and right. Politics has become a full-time profession rather than a part-time affair. Most of those who enter the field today expect to spend their entire careers there, and they surround themselves with other political professionals such as speechwriters, media consultants, pollsters, and spin doctors. Citizens have become increasingly aware that their representatives and rulers live in an entirely different and self-referential world. Voting preferences are now based less on class, sector, and professional interests and more on individualistic concerns about personal lifestyles, ethical convictions, and the role of government.

If all that were not enough, citizens—many of whom now have access through the Internet to vast sources of independent and critical information—have become better educated and more skeptical about the motives and behavior of their politicians. Moreover, enormous flows of South-North migration have so altered the demographic composition of most really existing democracies that a substantial share of their populations have no citizen rights or prospects for gaining them. This growing diversity challenges the notion of a common *demos* with a shared fate and hence a mutually accepted sense of the public good. Notwithstanding the current populist resistance to ethnic pluralism, really existing democracies will have to find a way to accommodate diversity and reform their institutions accordingly.

More conjunctural factors are also supposed to have played an important role. First and foremost, the collapse of Soviet-style "people's democracy" has deprived Western democracies of one of their primary bases of legitimacy—namely, their superiority over their communist rivals. Since the end of the Cold War, the democracies of the West have had to satisfy the more demanding criteria of equality, access, participation, and freedom promised by democratic ideals. The latest wave (which, *pace* Huntington, is not the "third wave") of democratization, which began in 1974, also contributed to a general rise in expectations and unrealistic assertions about "the end of history." Neoliberal reforms failed to produce their promise of continuous growth, fair distribution, and automatic equilibration, leading by 2008 to the Great Recession, which many democracies (especially in Europe) proved incapable of mitigating, much less resolving.

At the core of this consensus about crisis and decline lies the heavy emphasis that the practice of democracy places upon representation—especially via competition among political parties in regular and fair elections that are expected to produce, directly or indirectly, legitimate rulers.[1] Admittedly, parties have never been "loved" by citizens—partly because they are an overt expression of the interests and ideological cleavages that divide them but also because there is ample reason to suspect, as the German sociologist Robert Michels long ago asserted, that they are unusually susceptible to oligarchy and prone to self-serving corruption.[2]

In the face of such abundant evidence, convincing arguments, and massive consensus, how can anyone doubt that democracy is in decline?

SOME EMERGING EVIDENCE OF TRANSITION

From my perspective as a "card-carrying" transitologist, it should come as no surprise if I conclude that democracy is *not* in decline, but that it *is* in crisis and in the process of transition from one type to another[3]—although it is not at all clear what the new type (or types) will be or whether any new type will be an improvement over existing practices. Indeed, it is precisely this uncertainty about the rules of the game that is the predominant characteristic of all transitional situations. In generic terms, one might label this emerging configuration "post-liberal" (but definitely not "illiberal" or "anti-liberal"). Of course, this label does not convey much specificity of meaning, other than opening up the prospect for the outcome to be something qualitatively different.[4]

As is often the case with such debates, the answer hinges not on the facts but on the concepts and suppositions that determine which facts are salient and why. Not surprisingly, this begins with the definition of democracy that one uses. In 1991, Terry Karl and I proposed in these pages a very generic definition of democracy that involves neither specific institutions nor presupposed outcomes: "*Modern political democracy is a [regime] . . . in which rulers are held accountable for their actions in the public realm by citizens, [usually] acting indirectly through the competition and cooperation of their elected representatives.*"[5] I would now add for greater clarification: "*and in which citizens comply voluntarily with their rulers' decisions—even when they have not explicitly approved these decisions—because they regard them as having been taken legitimately.*"

In other words, democracy is a two-way process (or better, set of processes) in which citizens with equal political rights and obligations have at their disposal regular and reliable means to access information, demand justification, and apply sanctions on their rulers; in exchange, citizens accord these rulers legitimacy and agree to respect their decisions, even when disagreeing with them. This definition of democracy has two key implications for how we should determine whether democracy is in decline or in transition: This means that it would be a mistake (1) to focus exclusively on a single set of institutions (usually, the conduct of elections and the behavior of political parties) or (2) to make a judgment based on indicators of the substantive performance of a given democracy.

All that should count are the effectiveness of the processes of accountability and the willingness of citizens to accord legitimacy. Both can change for a variety of reasons, including the introduction of new communications technologies, the diffusion of novel ideals across borders, or the creation of new channels of representation. The core assumption is that if rulers know they will be held to account and if citizens believe their rulers to be legitimate, then the substantive outcomes will be satisfactory given the resources available. This definition implies that not all democracies should be held to the same standard of performance—for the simple reason that not all citizens will collectively want the same things and not all polities will be capable of producing the same level of public goods. Tocqueville famously argued that once democracy had established equality in the realms of politics and law, citizens would demand equality in social status and material wealth.[6] He was right about the tendency, but wrong about the eventual outcomes. Contemporary really existing democracies differ considerably and consistently in their distributive consequences.[7]

Another way of expressing this argument is that one should clearly separate the criteria for assessing the quality of *democracy* from those used to assess the quality of *government*. The former is about processes connecting the rulers to the ruled in ways that ensure mutual accountability, while the latter concerns the outcomes that ensue from the exercise of power, whether democratic or not. This implies the possibility that some autocracies could outperform some democracies—delivering, say, higher economic growth, lower inflation, better distribution of wealth, fuller employment, and in some cases even less corruption, stricter observance of the rule of law, and greater protection of human (but not civil) rights. Much of the anecdotal evidence for decline involves how governments—more and more of which admittedly belong to democratic regimes—are performing, not how democracy as such is doing.

SOME EMERGING EVIDENCE OF REFORM

About a decade ago, Alexander Trechsel and I put together for the Council of Europe a working group of academics and politicians on the theme "The Future of Democracy in Europe." During the ensuing discussions, the participants quickly became aware that there was a great deal of both political imagination and actual experimentation with regard to institutional reforms.[8] Much of this thinking and effort had gone largely unobserved because it was taking place at the local level or in a more or less sporadic fashion. In the case of newer democracies, pervasive disparagement of the intrinsic deficits of their regimes—that their democracies were "flawed," "partial," "hybrid," "pseudo," "façade," "illiberal," "stalled," "low-intensity," "delegative," "defective," or merely "electoral"—obscured the fact that they were often engaging in innovative practices.[9]

To the best of my knowledge there exists no complete inventory of these reform efforts. To list them all and attach them to their specific sites would greatly exceed the space accorded to me (as well as my expertise). Thus, I will simply offer readers a representative sample and invite them to pursue the task in a more systematic fashion:[10]

1. Referendums and initiatives are probably the most widely and frequently used innovation, as the kinds of issues that have become subject to such measures at both the national and subnational levels have proliferated. Granted, some of these referendums and initiatives are merely consultative, and many require a high threshold to become valid; nevertheless, they have given citizens in many polities a much more direct channel of participation in decision making than they had in the past.

2. "Participatory budgeting" is one reform that has been extensively studied since it was first implemented in Porto Alegre, Brazil, and then spread across several continents. Participatory budgeting involves convoking an assembly of self-selected or randomly chosen citizens to debate the distribution of some proportion of a governmental unit's total budget. A wide array of such forums have emerged over time, and their terminology differs—for example, "consensus conferencing," "citizens' panels," "citizens' juries," "planning cells," "issue forums," "citizens' assemblies," even "deliberation day"—as do the rules that govern them, but the intent is the same: to bring ordinary citizens closer to the policy-making process by personal participation.

3. The party primary, a device for selecting from among candidates competing for a political party's nomination, had long been a peculiarity of US politics. In recent decades, this practice has invaded other countries and continents. The modalities differ, but in generic terms primaries give party members (or even ordinary citizens) the capacity to penetrate firmly entrenched party oligarchies. Some places have even opted for "open primaries," in which candidates of all parties compete and the top two vote-getters, regardless of party affiliation, become the nominees for the general election. Another reform that could affect *partitocrazia* is the introduction of NOTA ("None of the Above") as an alternative choice on the ballot. In some versions, if a sufficient number of citizens check this box, the election has to be held again.

4. Public funding for political parties is yet another relatively recent innovation—one that has spread from Europe's really existing democracies to newer ones. The presumed objective is to counter the tendency toward disproportionate contributions from wealthy citizens and private corporations by shifting the burden to compulsory contributions from taxpayers as a whole. This usually involves some distribution formula based on the previous electoral results, which would seem to reinforce

incumbent advantage and, hence, oligarchy. Because the monitoring of these funds is often deficient and their receipt does not preclude the raising of additional funds from private sources, they have been a persistent source of corruption allegations.

5. In recent decades, quotas for women electoral candidates or even as members of the legislature have become almost standard in many really existing democracies. In some places, this is a formal legal obligation, even a provision of the national constitution. Elsewhere, political parties have adopted the practice voluntarily—at first mostly left-leaning parties, but increasingly parties in the center and on the right as well. Meanwhile, some countries have simply legislated that one-half or some lower proportion of seats in the legislature be reserved for women. An additional measure, called "zipping," requires electoral lists to order male and female candidates alternately. Efforts to promote gender parity have spread to the process of government formation as well: the informal practice of appointing women to head half of all ministries is becoming a norm. Less common is the notion that other social minorities that historically have suffered discrimination—ethnic, linguistic, or religious—should benefit from similar policies.

6. The devolution of greater powers to subnational political units is becoming more common. Most newly established democracies and several well-established West European democracies have recently transferred considerable decision-making authority to regions, provinces, or municipalities that had previously been ruled by their respective central governments. While full-scale federalism seems to be on the decline, this more flexible form of decentralization should allow citizens to hold their local governments more accountable.

7. Efforts to plan for the future have blossomed in response to the frequent complaint that really existing democracies are intrinsically "short-sighted"—tied to the electoral cycle or to

immediate expressions of public opinion and thus incapable of engaging in "forward thinking" or anticipating future problems and preventing their negative impact. Recent decades have witnessed a virtual explosion of "future commissions"—some within governments, others in think tanks or NGOs. It has become increasingly obligatory for legislative proposals and referendums to be accompanied by an expert evaluation of their eventual costs and consequences. In Hungary, there is even an "Ombudsman for Future Generations" who performs this task on a regular basis.

8. The proliferation of freedom-of-information acts all over the world has helped to keep citizens better informed about the behavior of their rulers. These laws give individual citizens and civic associations access to the material that governments have collected—even to material that is currently being used in the decision-making process. To be sure, members of the general public may not always possess the time or skill to mine these documents, the sheer volume of which has increased exponentially over the years with the increase in government surveillance. Nevertheless, such laws make a modest contribution toward ensuring the transparency upon which accountability rests.
9. New innovations in information and communications technology (ICT) are beginning to have a significant impact on the practice of democracy. Their low cost and broad distribution, as well as the personal anonymity that they offer, have given citizens access to sources of information that are difficult for established authorities to control or censor, and that frequently reveal behavior that rulers would rather keep secret. Parties and politicians have also felt compelled to use this technology to connect with their followers. Some parties and candidates have even used it effectively to raise funds and mobilize followers. Meanwhile, vast segments of civil society have made use of ICT to assemble "virtual" units of collective action that are often critical of established authorities.

10. The next steps in this technological transformation have already appeared in a few selected sites—namely, the use of electronic communications to influence the nomination of candidates and the formation of party programs, to match voters' personal preferences with the positions of parties and candidates (so-called smart voting), and finally to actually cast one's vote. Several countries have extended this form of "e-democracy" into "e-government" by setting up kiosks or bureaus where citizens can contact government agencies, download forms, and make complaints.

11. A few countries have introduced a novel system for funding civil society. Citizens can choose to allocate a fixed percentage of their tax obligations to an organization (or organizations) of their choice from among an approved list of associations, institutions, or agencies. Such organizations thus become compelled to compete publicly and vigorously for these funds by disclosing what they have been doing and propose to do in the future. Not only is the distribution of these funds an important financial resource for them, but it also serves as a proximate indicator of their legitimacy and reveals otherwise hidden citizen preferences.

12. The nature of citizenship—that most basic of democratic institutions—is beginning to change. There is a trend toward lowering the age of political maturity to sixteen. Nationals living abroad are able to vote at their respective embassies or consulates. Legally resident foreigners are gaining some voting and consultative rights in the countries where they live (especially at the local level), and in some places it has become easier for them to acquire citizenship in their new home countries. The true breakthrough will come when nationality, whether *jus sanguinis* or *jus soli,* is separated from the status of citizenship. There is even a de jure status for "supranational" citizenship in the European Union, and the diffusion of human and civic rights across national borders and their (admittedly erratic) enforcement by

international or regional courts have created a more extensive de facto system of citizen protection.

13. Representation by lot is one device that is hardly new. It was present at the founding of *demokratia* in ancient Athens. As mentioned above, some of the direct consultation of citizens on policy matters has involved the random sampling of participants from those physically present in a given constituency. A more indirect technique has been to assemble a random sample of citizens, register their initial opinions, subject them to a discussion of alternative points of view, test them for potential changes in opinion, and then publicize the results. The assembling of such "deliberative mini-publics" for "interactive polling" has become a common practice in Western democracies—although its practical impact on either policy content or political legitimacy has yet to be conclusively demonstrated (which, incidentally, is the case with many of the innovations presented above).

14. According to the orthodox view of democracy, representatives owe their legitimacy to having been elected in some regular, competitive, and honest fashion. Yet there has been an extraordinary increase in the number of nonelected persons claiming this status on the basis of their professional or organizational expertise, their appealing personality, their commitment to shared norms, or even their celebrity—and there is abundant evidence that many of them are accepted as such. Hardly a single leader of a civil society organization or social movement owes his or her position to a competitive electoral process, not to mention the movie stars and rock musicians who speak on behalf of worthy causes and whole continents.

So far, almost every one of these institutional experiments has focused on reviving *vertical accountability* through political parties or elections or *oblique accountability* through interest associations, social movements, or communications networks. Liberal versions of democratic theory, however, place a distinctive emphasis on *horizontal accountability.* Guided by the more general principle that really existing democracies are better off protecting citizens from tyranny than empowering them to act collectively, such checks and balances within the decision-making apparatus are intended to reduce the potential threat posed by mass citizen mobilization.

The three traditional sites of horizontal accountability—the executive, the legislature, and the judiciary—have experienced a rebalancing. Legislatures have tended to decline, executive power has varied according to the policy agenda (with the conduct of war being one of the major incentives for its growth), and judges (especially appellate judges) have greatly increased their powers. This process of constitutional juridification has varied considerably, with the United States providing an extreme case at the national level and the EU creating an entirely new layer of authority at the supranational level.

15. The establishment of a variety of "guardian institutions" is truly novel. Such institutions hardly existed before, and where they did, they played a much more subordinate role, but they now provide a wide variety of potential checks on decisions made by elected officials or legislators.[11] First and foremost among such institutions are independent central banks, which are authorized practically to dictate economic and financial policy. No democracy seems to be capable of doing without them. The central banks have been joined by an extraordinary array of national "independent regulatory agencies." In addition to the older ones, which regulated interstate commerce, transportation, public health, worker safety, food products, drugs, professional ethics, consumer protection, and the like, we now find electoral commissions, human-rights tribunals, and anticorruption agencies. These have all been deliberately "chartered" in such a way as to avoid political interference (in other words, democracy) and handed over to experts who will not bend to pressure from citizens or rulers or be captured by those whom they are supposed to regulate. If this were not enough,

these efforts are often seconded by global institutions such as the World Bank, the International Monetary Fund, the World Trade Organization, and innumerable other standard-setting and standard-enforcing institutions. The EU has not only its own central bank but also more than thirty regulatory agencies. No wonder citizens complain that they have no effective influence over policy; their politicians can hide behind this screen of supranational actors and pretend that they have no choice but to obey Washington, Brussels, or wherever.

No clear pattern emerges from the reform efforts sketched above, except that it appears not to be true that the practice of liberalism—political or economic—will inexorably produce a satisfying and stable equilibrium. So far, there is none in sight. In some cases, there are traces of "pre-liberal" democracy, with its enhanced role for direct citizen participation and occasional use of selection by lot. In others, especially in the devolution of territorial authority and the emphasis on freedom of information, one might be led to conclude that "more liberal" democracy is emerging, especially when these practices are combined with such substantive measures as the widespread deregulation of commercial and financial transactions, stronger protections for property rights, and the dismantling or downgrading of various policies of social protection.

Yet most of the reforms hint at a novel configuration that might be called "post-liberal."[12] Such a configuration would be rooted in the extension of public consultation on policy and budgeting issues, broader definitions of citizenship, public financing of political parties and citizen-chosen civil society organizations, quotas for women, "guardian institutions" designed to protect citizens from fraud and exploitation, the creation of "future commissions" to examine the potential impact of government decisions, and (why not?) the proliferation of self-selected persons claiming to represent a wider diversity of causes and places.[13]

Another, less obvious characteristic of this emerging type of democracy is its ambiguous attachment to the national state. Much of what this form of democracy is seeking to accomplish would require passive consent or active cooperation across its borders, up to and including the formation of supranational norms and institutions. The maxim that really existing democracy can only be practiced within really existing national states seems destined to be challenged.

Any alternative to "really existing" liberal democracy—except perhaps for more liberal and less democratic rule—is bound to be plagued by serious problems of "agency." However intellectually appealing this alternative may seem, it is usually impossible *ex ante* to specify which actors (or what combination thereof) would support such changes, how much of the transition costs they would be willing to bear, and how the reforms might be successfully and democratically implemented. Once a revolutionary rupture with the previous institutions and practices of liberal democracy has been ruled out—as seems to be the case for the foreseeable future—it is hard to see the potential basis for the sort of sustained social or political support that any combined and persistent reformist campaign would need. So far, all one can observe is a series of isolated and tentative efforts—many of which have yet to make much of a difference. It is almost impossible to overestimate the enormous entropy built into the institutions and practices of today's really existing democracies and the attendant difficulty in persuading people to accept new ideas about rather fundamental political and economic relations.

The earlier reforms presently embedded in liberal democracy were the product of efforts to close an enlarged gap between the ideal expectations and the real performance experienced by citizens, but they almost always required at least the specter, if not the imminent threat, of revolution to make the effort seem worthwhile. Today, however, revolutionaries are rare, and their terrorist replacements strengthen rather than weaken the will to retain the status quo. The actors who are presently challenging the performance and the legitimacy of really existing democracy are not its declared enemies; they are its avowed supporters. In other words, they are citizens and groups who believe that they are improving democracy, although they have no coherent plan for doing so. Indeed, the task of reform would be facilitated greatly if extremists on either the right or left were self-avowedly seeking to replace liberal rules and practices with some other form of government, but their efforts are presently inconsequential and unconvincing, and in my opinion they are likely to remain so.

As long as the greatest threats to democracy are coming from its "normal practitioners"—voters, citizens, deputies, special interests, movement activists, and "prominent personalities" engaging in their normatively sanctioned behaviors, it will be far more difficult to convince such actors of the necessity for a comprehensive package of institutional reforms. Contrary to past history, when such political transformations occurred only if a dedicated group advocating a plausible alternative existed and succeeded in imposing its model, all that most citizens experience in their daily lives today are "symptoms of morbidity" à la Gramsci—a lot of grumbling, dissatisfaction, powerlessness, and suboptimality, but hardly enough to motivate them to invest in a novel, ill-defined, and as yet untested model of post-liberal democracy.

NOTES

This is an essay in "practical political theory," not one of political science. It is my tentative effort to capture a complex set of interrelated phenomena in excessively general terms and without the requisite empirical references. I am grateful to the *Journal of Democracy* for its indulgence.

1. For a more detailed analysis of the shrinking role of political parties in really existing democracies, see Philippe C. Schmitter, "Parties Are Not What They Once Were," in Larry Diamond and Richard Gunther, eds., *Political Parties and Democracy* (Baltimore: Johns Hopkins University Press, 2001), 67–89.
2. Robert Michels, *Political Parties: A Sociological Study of Oligarchical Tendencies of Modern Democracy* (1911; New York: Crowell-Collier, 1962). More recently, his "Iron Law of Oligarchy" has been rebaptized by the Italians as "*partitocrazia*," an expression that has rapidly diffused throughout the political universe.
3. Three non-transitologists have arrived at the same conclusion: In their

introduction to *The Future of Representative Democracy* (Cambridge: Cambridge University Press, 2011), 17, editors Sonia Alonso, John Keane, and Wolfgang Merkel point out that several authors in the volume suggest that "what we are witnessing is not so much a crisis of representative democracy as its transformation into something new." Admittedly, I was a participant in this research group and, hence, one of the authors. Subsequently, however, a distinguished political theorist has arrived at the same conclusion quite independently, as I discovered after writing this essay: Alessandro Ferrara, "Judging Democracy in the Twenty-First Century: Crisis or Transformation?" *NoFo* 10 (2013), *www.helsinki.fi/nofo/NoFo10FERRARA.pdf.*

4. This has already happened several times in the past. The root concept of democracy persists, but its translation into rules and practices has been subject to three successive "revolutions," to use the expression of Robert Dahl; see his *Polyarchy* (New Haven: Yale University Press, 1971). For an extension of this argument to include five subsequent revolutions within really existing democracies, see Philippe C. Schmitter, "The Future of 'Real Existing' Democracy," European University Institute (unpubl. ms., 2007).
5. Philippe C. Schmitter and Terry Lynn Karl, "What Democracy Is . . . and Is Not," *Journal of Democracy* 2 (Summer 1991): 75–88. This essay has been widely reprinted in several languages.
6. In the first volume of his *Democracy in America,* Tocqueville makes this one of his founding observations about democracy: "The gradual development of equality of conditions is therefore a providential fact, and it has the principal characteristics of one: it is universal, it is enduring, each day it escapes human power; all events, like all men, serve its development"; see Alexis de Tocqueville, *Democracy in America,* trans. and ed. Harvey C. Mansfield and Delba Winthrop (Chicago: University of Chicago Press, 2000), 1:6. In the second volume, published some five years later, Tocqueville expresses some doubts about the impact of this "providential fact" and envisages the possibility of the development of an industrial aristocracy in America and even of an eventual despotism (2:530–34, 661–65).
7. Looking over the abundant literature on the "quality of democracy," one is impressed by the extent to which it presumes that the features of the Scandinavian democracies are universally appreciated and therefore occupy a prominent place among its criteria for excellence. Is it really a relevant question to ask why Brazil has not attained the standards of, say, Sweden—or even if Brazilians wish to become Swedish?

8. Philippe C. Schmitter and Alexander H. Trechsel, eds., *The Future of Democracy in Europe: Trends, Analyses, and Reforms* (Strasbourg: Council of Europe, 2004).
9. I am indebted to Leonardo Avritzer for my awareness of this and for his research, which demonstrates that the flow of innovations is not exclusively from really existing democracies to newly existing ones. The latter have much to contribute to the former.
10. For a more extensive list of potential as well as actual reforms, see Schmitter and Trechsel, *Future of Democracy,* which offers 29 of them.
11. See Robert Dahl, *Democracy and Its Critics* (New Haven: Yale University Press, 1989) for the initial observation.
12. For this distinction between "pre-liberal," "more liberal" and "post-liberal," see Philippe C. Schmitter, "Democracy's Future: More Liberal, Pre-Liberal, or Post-Liberal?," *Journal of Democracy* 6 (January 1995): 15–22.
13. For my very tentative effort at imagining what such a post-liberal democracy might eventually look like, see "The Prospect of Post-Liberal Democracy," in Karl Hinrichs, Herbert Kitschelt, and Helmut Wiesenthal, eds., *Kontingenz und Krise. Institutionenpolitik in kapitalistischen und postsozialistischen Gesellschaften. Claus Offe zu seinem 60. Geburtstag* (Frankfurt: Campus, 2000); "Un esbozo del posible aspecto de una democracia 'post-liberal,'" in Jose Felix Tezanos, ed., *Clase, estatus y poder en las sociedades emergentes: Quinto foro sobre tendencias sociales* (Madrid: Fundación Sistema, 2002), 587–98.

4

The Myth of Democratic Recession

STEVEN LEVITSKY AND LUCAN WAY

A near consensus has emerged that the world has fallen into a "democratic recession." Leading observers and democracy advocates characterize the last decade as a period of democratic "rollback," "erosion," or "decline,"[1] in which new democracies have fallen victim to a "powerful authoritarian undertow."[2] In an article entitled "The Great Democracy Meltdown," for example, Joshua Kurlantzick claims that global freedom has "plummeted."[3] Another observer suggests that "we might in fact be seeing the beginning of the end for democracy."[4]

The gloomy mood is made manifest in Freedom House's yearly reports in the *Journal of Democracy*. Summarizing Freedom House's annual survey of freedom, Arch Puddington warned in 2006 of a growing "pushback against democracy,"[5] characterized 2007 and 2008 as years of democratic "decline,"[6] claimed that the democratic erosion had "accelerated" in 2009,[7] and described global democracy as "under duress" in 2010.[8] Following a brief moment of optimism during the Arab Spring, Freedom House warned of a democratic "retreat" in 2012 and an "authoritarian resurgence" in 2013.[9]

This is a gloomy picture indeed. It is not, however, an accurate one. There is little evidence that the democratic sky is falling or (depending on your choice of fable) that the wolf of authoritarian resurgence has arrived.[10] The state of global democracy has remained stable over the last decade, and it has improved markedly relative to the 1990s. Perceptions of a democratic recession, we argue, are rooted in a flawed understanding of the events of the early 1990s. The excessive optimism and voluntarism that pervaded analyses of early post–Cold War transitions generated unrealistic expectations that, when not realized, gave rise to exaggerated pessimism and gloom. In fact, despite increasingly unfavorable global conditions in recent years, new democracies remain strikingly robust.

THE EMPIRICAL RECORD

A look at the empirical record suggests little or no evidence of a democratic recession. We compared the scores of four prominent global democracy indices: Freedom House, Polity, the Economist Intelligence Unit, and the Bertelsmann democracy index.[11] Table 1 shows each index's mean level of democracy (on a normalized scale from 0 to 1) from 2000 to 2013. All four indices' mean democracy scores *remained the same or increased* during this period. According to leading democracy indices such as Freedom House and Polity, then, the world is more democratic today than it was in 2000 (and considerably more democratic than it was in 1990 or any year prior to that). Even if we take the mid-2000s—often cited as the beginning of the democratic recession—as our starting point, three of the four indices show either no change or a slight improvement.[12] Only Freedom House shows a decline between 2005 and 2013, and that decline (from 0.63 to 0.62) is extremely modest.

If we examine the overall number of democracies in the world, the data similarly suggest stability rather than decline. Table 2 shows the four indices' scores for the absolute number of democracies as

TABLE 1. Mean Democracy score for the world according to four surveys

	1990	2000	2001	2002	2003	2004	2005	2006	2007	2008	2009	2010	2011	2012	2013
Freedom House	0.53	0.59	0.59	0.61	0.61	0.62	0.63	0.63	0.63	0.62	0.62	0.62	0.62	0.61	0.62
Polity IV	0.53	0.65	0.66	0.66	0.67	0.67	0.68	0.69	0.69	0.69	0.69	0.69	0.70	0.70	0.71
Economist Intelligence Unit	—	—	—	—	—	—	—	0.55	—	0.55	—	0.55	0.55	0.55	0.55
Bertelsmann Index	—	—	—	—	—	—	0.53	—	0.54	—	0.54	—	0.53	—	0.53

Note: All indices are rescaled to the 0–1 interval. Freedom House political-rights and civil-liberties scores are averaged and reversed.

well as the percentage of the world's regimes that were fully democratic between 2000 and 2013. Again, Freedom House and Polity show an increase in the number of democracies since 2000. Only if we look at the 2005–13 period do we see any decline, and that decline is very modest. Freedom House shows a drop-off of *one* democracy between 2005 and 2013. The pattern is similar with respect to the percentage of democracies in the world: both Freedom House and Polity show a decline of one percentage point between 2005 and 2013.

As an additional measure, we examined all cases of significant regime change—defined as countries whose Freedom House scores increased or decreased by three points or more—between 1999 and 2013.Whereas 23 countries experienced a significant improvement in their Freedom House score between 1999 and 2013, only 8 experienced a significant decline. Even between 2005 and 2013, the number of significantly improved cases (10) exceeded the number of significant decliners (8). Moreover, most of the significant declines occurred not in democracies but in regimes that were *already authoritarian*, such as the Central African Republic, Gambia, Guinea-Bissau, and Jordan.

Indeed, what is most striking about the 2000–13 period is how

TABLE 2. Percentage and absolute number of democracies according to four surveys

	1990	2000	2001	2002	2003	2004	2005	2006	2007	2008	2009	2010	2011	2012	2013
Freedom House	39%	45%	44%	46%	46%	46%	46%	47%	47%	46%	46%	45%	45%	46%	45%
	65	86	85	89	88	89	89	90	90	89	89	87	87	90	88
Polity IV	39%	50%	52%	53%	53%	56%	58%	58%	57%	58%	57%	57%	59%	58%	57%
	56	80	83	85	84	90	93	95	92	95	93	93	96	94	94
Economist Intelligence Unit	—	—	—	—	—	—	—	49%	—	48%	—	47%	47%	47%	47%
	—	—	—	—	—	—	—	82	—	80	—	79	78	79	78
Bertelsmann Index	—	—	—	—	—	—	55%	—	64%	—	62%	—	61%	—	59%
	—	—	—	—	—	—	65	—	76	—	74	—	72	—	70

few democracies actually broke down. Seven countries that Freedom House classified as Free in the late 1990s are no longer classified as Free today: Bolivia, Ecuador, Honduras, Mali, the Philippines, Thailand, and Venezuela.[13] Of these seven cases, the scores for Ecuador, Bolivia, and the Philippines declined only marginally, and all three regimes remained borderline democracies in 2014 (indeed, the Philippines has redemocratized; Freedom House's decision to designate it as Partly Free appears to reflect problems of corruption, *not* violations of democratic rules of the game). Honduras and Mali suffered military coups in 2009 and 2012, respectively, but both authoritarian turns were subsequently reversed.[14] That leaves Thailand and Venezuela as the only unambiguously democratic regimes that collapsed and remained authoritarian in 2014.

The list of breakdowns could be expanded to include Nicaragua and Sri Lanka, two near-democracies (classified as Partly Free by Freedom House in the late 1990s) that deteriorated into authoritarianism in the 2000s. One might also add Hungary (still classified as Free by Freedom House in 2013), although it remains, at worst, a borderline case. Turkey, which is sometimes labeled a case of democratic breakdown, underwent a transition from one hybrid regime to another. Although the AKP government has shown clear authoritarian tendencies, the regime that preceded it—marked by vast military influence, restrictions on Kurdish and Islamist parties, and substantial media repression—was never democratic (in fact, Turkey's Freedom House score in 2013 was better than it was prior to the AKP's first election victory in 2002).

Even if we categorized all these cases as democratic breakdowns, despite most of them being borderline cases (Bolivia, Ecuador, Hungary, the Philippines) or cases in which authoritarian turns were subsequently reversed (Honduras, Mali, the Philippines), the number of breakdowns is matched by cases of democratic advance. Eight countries—including some very important ones—entered Freedom House's Free category in the 2000s and remain there today: Brazil, Croatia, Ghana, Indonesia, Mexico, Peru, Senegal, and Serbia.[15] This list does not include countries, such as Chile, that were already classified as Free but experienced major democratic advances (in the Chilean case, the establishment of full civilian control over the military). Nor does it include countries such as Nepal, Pakistan, or Tunisia, which became considerably more democratic after the mid-2000s but remained in Freedom House's Partly Free category.

The big picture over the last decade, then, is one of net stability. Although it is certainly possible to identify cases of democratic backsliding, the existence of an equal or greater number of democratic advances belies any notion of a global democratic "meltdown." As tables 1 and 2 make clear, the net change since the mid-2000s is essentially zero. Thailand, Venezuela, and perhaps Hungary are suffering democratic recessions. But claims of a worldwide democratic downturn lack empirical foundation.

THE ILLUSION OF BACKSLIDING

Why do many observers perceive there to be a democratic recession when the evidence for such a recession is so thin? The global regime landscape looks darkened today because observers viewed the events of the initial post–Cold War period through rose-tinted glasses. During the early 1990s, many observers slipped into an excessively optimistic—even teleological—mindset in which virtually all forms of authoritarian crisis or regime instability were conflated with democratization.[16]

The excessive optimism of the early 1990s was shaped, in part, by the extraordinarily successful democratizations of the early "third-wave" period (1974–89). In Southern Europe (Greece, Spain, Portugal), South America (Argentina, Brazil, Chile, Uruguay), and Central Europe (Bulgaria, Czechoslovakia, Hungary, Poland), authoritarian crises consistently led to democratization. Initial authoritarian openings almost invariably escaped the control of regime elites and evolved into full-scale transitions. And when authoritarian regimes fell, they were almost invariably replaced by democracies.

In retrospect, it is clear that these early third-wave transitions differed markedly from later transitions in Africa and the former Soviet Union. Transitions in Southern Europe, South America, and Central Europe occurred under conditions that favored successful democratization, including relatively high levels of development, robust civic and opposition movements, functioning states, and extensive ties to the West. Yet observers generalized from these cases, drawing at least two false lessons that powerfully shaped the way that they interpreted the transitions of the 1990s.[17]

First, observers began to conflate authoritarian breakdown with democratization. The collapse of a dictatorship may yield diverse outcomes, ranging from democracy (post-1989 Poland) to the establishment of a new authoritarian regime (post-1979 Iran) to state collapse and anarchy (post-2011 Libya). Historically, in fact, most authoritarian breakdowns have *not* brought democratization.[18] Thus, although the collapse of a dictatorship creates opportunities for democratization, there are no theoretical or empirical bases for assuming such an outcome. Yet that is exactly what many observers did in the 1990s. Wherever dictatorships fell and opposition groups ascended to power, transitions were described as democratization and subsequent regimes were labeled "new democracies."

Second, all authoritarian openings were assumed to mark the onset of a transition that would eventually lead to democracy. Thus even limited openings aimed at deflecting international pressure were expected to escape the control of autocrats and take on a life of their own, as had occurred in countries such as Brazil, Chile, Hungary, Poland, and Spain. Such expectations ignored the fact that autocrats may (and often do) undertake "window-dressing" reforms aimed at defusing short-term crises and then use their continued control of the army, police, and major revenue sources to reconsolidate power once the crisis has passed.

The tendency to conflate authoritarian crisis and democratic transition was powerfully reinforced by the demise of communism. The fall of the Berlin Wall and the collapse of the Soviet Union generated a widespread perception that liberal democracy was the "only game in town." Because all roads seemed to lead to democracy, observers began to interpret all regime crises as incipient democratic transitions.

This excessively optimistic mindset led observers to mischaracterize many post–Cold War regime crises. Although the 1990s are widely viewed as a decade of unprecedented democratization, they are more accurately described as a period of unprecedented authoritarian crisis. The end of the Cold War posed an enormous challenge to autocrats. Both Soviet client states and Western-backed anticommunist dictatorships lost external support. Western democracies emerged as the dominant center of military and economic power, and the United States and the European Union began to promote democracy to an unprecedented degree. At the same time, deep economic crises deprived autocrats of the resources needed to sustain themselves in power. States were effectively bankrupted throughout much of Africa and the former Soviet Union, leaving governments unable to pay their soldiers, police, and bureaucrats. In many cases (Albania, Benin, Cambodia, Georgia, Haiti, Liberia, Madagascar, Tajikistan, Zaire), states either collapsed or were brought to the brink of collapse.

Conditions in the early 1990s thus amounted to a virtual

"perfect storm" for dictatorships. Throughout Africa, the former Soviet Union, and elsewhere, autocrats confronted severe fiscal crises, weak or collapsing states, and intense international pressure for multiparty elections.

Lacking resources, external allies, or reliable coercive institutions, many of these autocracies fell into severe crisis. The result was widespread "pluralism by default,"[19] in which competition—and even turnover—occurred because governments lacked even rudimentary means to suppress opposition challenges. Autocrats fell from power in Albania, Belarus, Benin, the Central African Republic, Congo-Brazzaville, Georgia, Madagascar, Malawi, Mali, Moldova, Niger, Ukraine, and Zaire, not because they faced robust democracy movements, but because they were bankrupt, their states were in disarray, and in many cases they had lost control of the coercive apparatus. Likewise, governments in Cambodia, Cameroon, Gabon, Kyrgyzstan, Mozambique, Russia, and elsewhere tolerated competitive multiparty elections because they lacked even minimal capacity to resist them.

These moments of authoritarian weakness and instability were widely equated with democratization. Thus the ascent of noncommunists to power in Russia and other post-Soviet states, as well as the fall of autocrats in Madagascar, Malawi, Niger, Zambia, and other African states, were frequently characterized as democratic transitions. Similarly, the holding of multiparty elections in Angola, Cambodia, Cameroon, Gabon, Guinea-Bissau, Kenya, Mozambique, and Tanzania was said to mark the onset of democratic transitions, however "flawed" or "prolonged." Nearly all these regimes were characterized as "new democracies" or, at minimum, some diminished subtype of democracy (e.g., electoral, illiberal, unconsolidated).[20] This optimism was shared by Freedom House, which upgraded autocracies in Gabon, Jordan, Kazakhstan, Uzbekistan, and even totalitarian Turkmenistan to Partly Free status in the early 1990s.

Such evaluations were largely misguided. Many of the authoritarian crises of the early and mid-1990s did not constitute meaningful movement toward democracy. Numerous autocracies broke down because states either collapsed (e.g., Azerbaijan, Georgia, Sierra Leone, Tajikistan, Zaire) or weakened dramatically (e.g., Belarus, Madagascar, Malawi, Ukraine). State failure brings violence and instability; it almost never brings democratization. Many other regime "openings" were, in reality, moments of extraordinary incumbent weakness, driven not by societal pressure for democracy but rather by severe fiscal crisis, state weakness, or external vulnerability. For example, Russian politics were competitive in the early 1990s not because Boris Yeltsin presided over a democratic transition but because he presided over a state in disarray, which left him unable to control his own security forces, bureaucracy, and regional governments. Likewise, Cambodia's competitive 1993 elections were a product of the virtual state collapse that followed Vietnamese and Soviet withdrawal. Bankruptcy and international isolation compelled the Hun Sen government to cede control of the electoral process to the UN. Similarly, autocrats in Cameroon and Gabon, facing severe fiscal crises, riots, and the specter of international isolation, were compelled to hold unusually competitive elections in the early 1990s.

For observers who viewed these and other cases of pluralism by default as democratic transitions, the developments of the 2000s were bound to be disappointing. The "perfect storm" conditions of the initial post–Cold War period eventually passed. First, the economies of most developing countries improved during the 1990s, and thanks to soaring commodity prices, many of them boomed in the 2000s. Consequently, governments that a decade earlier had lacked funds to maintain patronage networks or even pay soldiers and bureaucrats were now flush with resources—helping to restore a minimum of state capacity.

Second, autocrats adapted to the post–Cold War environment. Rulers whose ignorance of how to survive in a context of multiparty elections nearly cost them power in the early 1990s eventually learned how to manage competitive elections, coopt rivals and independent media, control the private sector, and starve civic and opposition groups of resources without resorting to the kind of naked repression or fraud that could trigger a domestic legitimacy crisis and international isolation.[21]

Third, the geopolitical environment changed. The extraordinary influence of the United States and the EU, which had peaked in the immediate post–Cold War period, declined in the 2000s. At the same time, the emerging influence of China, Russia, and other regional powers, together with soaring oil prices, created more space for autocrats in Asia, the former Soviet Union, and Africa.

By the 2000s, economic recovery, state-rebuilding, and a more permissive international environment had reduced the level of authoritarian weakness and instability that had characterized much of Africa, the former Soviet Union, and Asia during the initial post–Cold War period. Less vulnerable to international pressure and with greater revenue and more effective states at their disposal, autocracies that had been highly vulnerable in the 1990s were, in many cases, able to reconsolidate power. In Cambodia, for example, improved finances and fading international pressure enabled the Hun Sen government to reestablish authoritarian dominance. Without the extreme fiscal and external constraints of the early 1990s, the ruling Cambodian People's Party was able to repress rivals and rig elections with greater impunity. Likewise, Presidents Paul Biya in Cameroon and Omar Bongo in Gabon reconsolidated power in the late 1990s and early 2000s, reversing earlier concessions—such as constitutional term limits—that many observers had interpreted as democratic "openings." Similar processes of authoritarian reconsolidation occurred in Algeria, Angola, Burma, Congo-Brazzaville, Mozambique, and elsewhere.

Much the same pattern could be observed in the former Soviet Union, where regimes that had been marked by weakness and instability during the initial postcommunist period consolidated during the 2000s. In Russia, for example, state-rebuilding and soaring oil prices allowed the Putin government to coopt the private sector and media, repress opponents, and manipulate elections to a degree that had been unthinkable a decade earlier.[22] In Belarus, the government of Alyaksandr Lukashenka established vast control over the economy during the second half of the 1990s, which allowed him to effectively starve his opponents of resources. Authoritarian regimes also consolidated in Armenia, Azerbaijan, and Tajikistan.

In sum, improved finances, state reconstruction, and a less hostile international environment enabled many authoritarian regimes that had been weak and unstable in the initial post–Cold War period to stabilize and even consolidate in the late 1990s and early 2000s. Unsurprisingly, countries such as Azerbaijan, Belarus, Cambodia, the Central African Republic, Congo-Brazzaville, Gabon, Guinea-Bissau, Jordan, Kazakhstan, Kyrgyzstan, Russia, Tajikistan, Turkmenistan, and Uzbekistan, all of which Freedom House had optimistically upgraded to Partly Free status in the early 1990s, were downgraded to Not Free.

These transitions from weak or unstable authoritarianism to more stable authoritarian rule are often viewed as cases of democratic failure and taken as evidence of a democratic recession. Such characterizations are misleading. Many of these regimes were never remotely democratic, and in some of them (e.g., Azerbaijan, Cambodia, Jordan, Kazakhstan, Tajikistan, Uzbekistan), democracy was never even seriously on the agenda. Just as authoritarian crisis should not be equated with democratic transition, authoritarian (re)consolidation should not be equated with democratic rollback.

In other cases, regime instability—often rooted in state failure—generated brief democratic "moments" in which intense international pressure or the extreme weakness of all major political actors permitted competitive elections and turnover (e.g., Bangladesh 1991; Haiti 1991; Congo-Brazzaville 1992; Belarus 1994; Niger 1999; Guinea-Bissau 2000; Madagascar 2002; Burundi 2005). Although these cases may have been minimally "democratic" on election day, they did not remain so after new governments took office—and thus could not be described as democratic regimes. Indeed, turnover occurred under conditions that overwhelmingly favored nondemocratic outcomes: democratic institutions existed only on parchment (in many cases, they had never been tested); states were weak or collapsing, resulting in pervasive neopatrimonialism and the absence of rule of law; private sectors were small and state-dependent; and civil societies and opposition parties were weak and disorganized. The combination of neopatrimonial states and impoverished societies gave incumbents vast resource advantages from day one, and in the absence of functioning democratic institutions, civil society, or an organized opposition, constraints on authoritarian abuse were minimal. Under such conditions, new governments almost inevitably abuse power, triggering either regime instability or another round of authoritarianism.

"Democratic moments" thus proved ephemeral, if not illusory, in each of the cases listed above. For example, Congo-Brazzaville experienced electoral turnover in 1992, but new president Pascal Lissouba immediately dissolved parliament and held flawed elections that triggered an opposition boycott and an eventual descent into civil war and dictatorship. Similarly, Burundi's competitive elections in 2005 led Freedom House to label it an "electoral democracy," but President Domitien Ndayizeye immediately began to arrest opposition leaders and journalists, and subsequent elections were marred by fraud and repression. In Guinea-Bissau, the 1999 overthrow of João Bernardo Vieira led to internationally sponsored elections won by opposition leader Kumba Yala (which led Freedom House to label the country an electoral democracy). But Yala was as authoritarian as his predecessor, closing newspapers and arresting opposition leaders and the president of the Supreme Court before his overthrow in a 2003 coup.

Newly elected presidents also immediately abused power in Bangladesh, Belarus, the Central African Republic, Haiti, Madagascar, Niger, and elsewhere. These regimes were never democracies in any meaningful sense, for any meaningful period of time. To label them as cases of subsequent "democratic breakdown" is, therefore, quite misleading. And yet most of the breakdowns cited by proponents of the democratic-recession thesis are precisely of this type—take the list of 25 post-2000 breakdowns in Larry Diamond's chapter in this book (see table on page 103).

Nearly two-thirds of these breakdowns were of regimes that (at best) were no more than ephemeral "democratic moments." If we limit our analysis to *actual democratic regimes*—defined, say, as those in which at least one democratically elected government held free elections and peacefully ceded power to an elected successor—16 of Diamond's 25 "democratic breakdowns" disappear. Of the nine cases of breakdown that remain,[23] only five still had authoritarian regimes in 2014, and one of those was a microstate.

NONDEMOCRATIZATION IN THE 2000s

Contemporary pessimism about the fate of global democracy is also rooted in excessive voluntarism. Many of those who argue that democracy is in retreat focus less on democratic backsliding than on the absence of democratic *progress*. In effect, nondemocratization in China, the Middle East, or Central Asia is treated as a setback. For example, Puddington's 2009 report in the *Journal of Democracy* claimed that "perhaps the most disappointing development" in Asia in 2008 was "the failure of China to enact significant democratic reforms . . . during its year as host of the Olympic Games."[24] The following year, he cited the Kazakh government's failure to undertake political reform as evidence of a "downward spiral" in Central Asia and pointed to the absence of political liberalization in Cuba as evidence of "continued erosion of freedom worldwide."[25] Puddington's most recent *Journal of Democracy* report openly cites unmet expectations—as opposed to *actual rollback*—as a source of democratic gloom, writing that although observers had "predicted that China would rather quickly evolve toward a more liberal and perhaps democratic system," the government instead developed new strategies "designed to maintain rigid one-party rule."[26]

The failure of authoritarian regimes in China, the Middle East, or Central Asia to democratize should not be taken as evidence of democratic retreat (doing so would be akin to taking a glass that is half full and declaring it not to be half empty but to be emptying out). Nor should it surprise us. By the mid-2000s, nearly every country with minimally favorable conditions for democracy had already democratized. With a handful of exceptions (e.g., Malaysia, Singapore, Thailand, Turkey, and now Venezuela), the low-hanging fruit had been picked. Today, most of the world's remaining non-democracies exist in countries that existing theory suggests are unlikely to democratize.[27]

According to a substantial body of research, stable democratization is unlikely in very poor countries with weak states (e.g., much of sub-Saharan Africa), dynastic monarchies with oil and Western support (e.g., the Persian Gulf States), and single-party regimes with strong states and high growth rates (China, Vietnam, Malaysia, Singapore). Our own research suggests that democratization is less likely in countries with very low linkage to the West (e.g., Central Asia, much of Africa) and in regimes born of violent revolution (China, Ethiopia, Eritrea, Vietnam, Cuba, Iran, Laos, North Korea). If we take seriously these lessons generated by several decades of research, relatively few countries today could be considered true democratic underperformers. While the recent stagnation in the overall number of democracies in the world may be normatively displeasing, it is entirely consistent with existing theory.

Why, then, has the lack of democratic expansion since the mid-2000s triggered so much pessimism and gloom? One reason is the unfounded expectations raised by the collapse of communism. After the extraordinary events of 1989–91, many observers simply assumed that the wave of democratic advances of the 1980s and 1990s would continue.

Another reason for contemporary disappointment is excessive voluntarism. The early third-wave democratizations dealt a powerful blow to the classic structuralist theories that had predominated in the 1960s and 1970s. These theories emphasized the social, economic, and cultural obstacles to democratization in the developing and communist worlds. Democratization in countries like Bolivia, El Salvador, Ghana, and Mongolia made it clear that democratization was possible anywhere. Yet this healthy skepticism regarding overly structuralist analysis evolved into exaggerated voluntarism.

Evidence that structural factors such as wealth, low inequality, or a robust civil society are not necessary for democratization led many observers to conclude that they are causally unimportant. In other words, the important lesson that democratization can happen anywhere was taken by some observers to mean that it *should happen everywhere*.

There are simply no theoretical or empirical bases for such expectations. A wealth of research has shown that structural factors such as level of development, inequality, economic performance, natural-resource wealth, state capacity, strength of civil society, and ties to the West continue to powerfully affect the likelihood of achieving and sustaining democracy. It is no coincidence that most of the world's remaining nondemocracies are clustered in the Middle East, sub-Saharan Africa, and the former Soviet Union. Many countries in these regions are characterized by multiple factors that scholars have associated with authoritarianism. One may hope (and work) for democratization in countries like Cambodia, Ethiopia, Kazakhstan, Libya, or Iraq, but *expectations* that democratization will occur in such cases lack theoretical or empirical foundation. And the dashing of unfounded expectations should not be confused with democratic recession.

DEMOCRACY'S SURPRISING RESILIENCE

Disappointment over the lack of democratization in countries where democracy is unlikely to emerge should not obscure the extraordinary democratic achievements of the last quarter-century. When the *Journal of Democracy* was launched in 1990, there were 38 developing and postcommunist countries classified as Free by Freedom House. In 2014, that number stood at 60.

As impressive as the breadth of the third wave has been its robustness. At the time of the *Journal of Democracy*'s inaugural issue, newly democratic regimes in Latin America and Central Europe were widely viewed as precarious. Scholars of democratization were skeptical that many of them would endure. In their classic book on transitions from authoritarian rule, for example, Guillermo O'Donnell and Philippe Schmitter characterized Latin American cases as "uncertain democracies."[28] Likewise, few scholars expected that the 1989 transitions in Central Europe would produce almost uniformly stable democratic regimes. Yet with a few short-lived exceptions (e.g., Peru, 1992–2000), the democracies that emerged in South America and Central Europe have now survived for a quarter-century or more. Moreover, they survived despite severe economic crises and radical economic reforms that many scholars believed were incompatible with democracy. Between 1990 and 2000, several other important countries democratized, including Croatia, Ghana, Indonesia, Mexico, Serbia, Slovakia, South Africa, and Taiwan. Although some of these new democracies were marked by deep racial or ethnic cleavages, they too proved strikingly robust.

These patterns did not change substantially after 2000. Democratic breakdowns remained rare, often short-lived, and generally unrepresentative of broader trends. Although democracy retreated in Sri Lanka, Thailand, and Venezuela, it survived in a range of important middle-income countries, including Argentina, Brazil, Chile, Colombia, Croatia, India, Indonesia, Mexico, Poland, Serbia, South Africa, South Korea, and Taiwan. Democracy also survived in several countries with strikingly unfavorable conditions, including Benin, the Dominican Republic, El Salvador, Ghana, Guyana, Mongolia, and Romania. These were countries with little or no democratic tradition, weak states, high levels of poverty and inequality, and in some cases deeply divided societies. Yet their democracies endured, and some of them are now more than two decades old.

In several important countries, democracy not only survived but *strengthened* during the 2000s. In Brazil, which suffered severe governability problems in the 1980s and early 1990s, the stability and quality of democracy improved markedly in the 2000s; in India, expanding rates of participation, particularly among poorer and lower-caste citizens, have created an increasingly inclusionary democracy; in Chile, a 2005 constitutional reform eliminated remaining authoritarian enclaves and established full civilian control over the military; in Croatia, Ghana, Mexico, and Taiwan, former authoritarian ruling parties returned to power and governed democratically—a critical step toward consolidation. And in Colombia and Poland, democratic institutions effectively checked the ambitions of autocratic-leaning presidents (Alvaro Uribe in Colombia, Lech Kaczyński in Poland). These were major democratic successes, many of which occurred in large and influential countries. Yet they received far less attention than democratic backsliding in Thailand and Venezuela and nondemocratization in China.

These successes suggest an alternative way of viewing the events of the 2000s. Over the last decade, several global developments posed a serious threat to new democracies. These included the severe post-2008 economic crisis in Western democracies, the declining influence of the United States and the European Union, the growing power and self-confidence of China and Russia, and soaring oil prices. Yet the number of actual democratic breakdowns has been strikingly low.

Arguably, then, the real story of the last decade is not democracy's "meltdown" but rather its resilience in the face of a darkening geopolitical landscape. This resilience merits further study. Understanding its sources may help democracy advocates to prepare for the day when the wolf of authoritarian resurgence does, in fact, arrive.

NOTES

1. See Larry Diamond, "The Democratic Rollback: The Resurgence of the Predatory State," *Foreign Affairs* 87 (March–April 2008): 36–48; Diamond, "Democracy's Deepening Recession," *Atlantic.com,* 2 May 2014; Arch Puddington, "The 2008 Freedom House Survey: A Third Year of Decline," *Journal of Democracy* 20 (April 2009): 93–107; Puddington, "The Freedom House Survey for 2009: The Erosion Accelerates," *Journal of Democracy* 21 (April 2010): 136–50; Joshua Kurlantzick, "The Great Democracy Meltdown," *New Republic,* 9 May 2011, 12–15, available at *tnr.com.*
2. Diamond, "Democratic Rollback," 36.
3. Kurlantzick, "Great Democracy Meltdown."

4. See Robert Battison, "The 'Democratic Recession' Has Turned into a Modern Zeitgeist of Democratic Reform," *OpenDemocracy* 21 (December 2011).
5. Arch Puddington, "The 2006 Freedom House Survey: The Pushback Against Democracy," *Journal of Democracy* 18 (April 2007): 125–37.
6. Puddington, "Third Year of Decline."
7. Puddington, "Erosion Accelerates."
8. Arch Puddington, "The Freedom House Survey for 2011: Democracy Under Duress," *Journal of Democracy* 22 (April 2011): 17–31.
9. Arch Puddington, "The Freedom House Survey for 2012: Breakthroughs in the Balance," *Journal of Democracy* 24 (April 2013): 49; Arch Puddington, "The Freedom House Survey for 2013: The Democratic Leadership Gap," *Journal of Democracy* 25 (April 2014): 90.
10. Jay Ulfelder makes a similar argument. See Ulfelder, "The Democratic Recession That *Still* Isn't," *http://dartthrowingchimp.wordpress.com/2014/01/23/the-democratic- recession-that-still-isnt*.
11. For Freedom House data, see *freedomhouse.org*; Polity data: *systemicpeace.org/polity/polity4.htm*; Economic Intelligence Unit data: *www.eiu.com/public/topical_report.aspx?campaignid=Democracy0814*; Bertelsmann data: *www.bti-project.org/index/*. All scores for actual years rather than year of report.
12. The Varieties of Democracy Index, which is not shown here, also finds no decline. See Staffan I. Lindberg et al., "V-Dem: A New Way to Measure Democracy," *Journal of Democracy* 25 (July 2014): 162–63.
13. We exclude microstates such as Fiji (which Freedom House classified as Free for one year in 1999 but which arguably never established a democratic regime) and Solomon Islands. Two other countries—Argentina and Guyana—briefly exited Freedom House's Free category during the 2000s but returned within one year.
14. Similarly, Ukraine (which was classified as Partly Free in the late 1990s but democratized in the mid-2000s) slid into competitive authoritarianism in 2010, but the regime collapsed in 2014.
15. Freedom House moved Mexico back into the Partly Free category in 2011 due to drug violence. However, there exists a broad scholarly consensus that Mexico retains a democratic regime. Senegal also slipped into the Partly Free category in the mid-2000s but regained its Free status in 2013.
16. For a similar critique, see Thomas Carothers, "The End of the Transition Paradigm," *Journal of Democracy* 13 (January 2002): 5–21; also Marc Howard and Meir R. Walters, "Mass Mobilization and the Democracy

Bias: A Comparison of Egypt and Ukraine," Georgetown University (unpubl. ms.).

17. See Carothers, "End of the Transition Paradigm."
18. See Milan Svolik, *The Politics of Authoritarian Rule* (New York: Cambridge University Press, 2012).
19. Lucan Way, "Pluralism by Default: Weak Autocrats and the Rise of Competitive Politics," University of Toronto (unpubl. ms.).
20. See David Collier and Steven Levitsky, "Democracy with Adjectives: Conceptual Innovation in Comparative Research," *World Politics* 49 (April 1997): 430–51.
21. Michael Bratton and Daniel Posner, "A First Look at Second Elections in Africa, with Illustrations from Zambia," in Richard A. Joseph, ed., *State, Conflict, and Democracy in Africa* (Boulder, CO: Lynne Rienner, 1999), 387; Lucan Way, "Deer in Headlights: Incompetence and Weak Authoritarianism After the Cold War," *Slavic Review* 71 (Fall 2012): 619–46.
22. See Mikhail Myagkov, Peter C. Ordeshook, and Dimitri Shakin, *The Forensics of Election Fraud: Russia and Ukraine* (New York: Cambridge University Press, 2009).
23. These are Venezuela and Thailand in 2005, Solomon Islands, Honduras, Philippines, Sri Lanka, Nicaragua, Ukraine, and Mali.
24. Puddington, "Third Year of Decline," 103.
25. Puddington, "Erosion Accelerates," 137, 141.
26. Puddington, "Democratic Leadership Gap," 90–91.
27. Marc F. Plattner, "The End of the Transitions Era?" *Journal of Democracy* 25 (July 2014): 5–16.
28. Guillermo O'Donnell and Philippe C. Schmitter, *Transitions from Authoritarian Rule: Tentative Conclusions About Uncertain Democracies* (Baltimore: Johns Hopkins University Press, 1986).

5

Democracy Aid at 25: Time to Choose

THOMAS CAROTHERS

With the twenty-fifth anniversary of the fall of the Berlin Wall so recently upon us, efforts to take stock of the global state of democracy have been proliferating. Efforts to take stock of the state of democracy aid, by contrast, have been a good deal rarer. Even though this type of international assistance has a specific goal—to foster and advance democratization—criteria for assessing it are elusive. "Democracy aid" itself is a catchall term for an endeavor that has acquired enough moving parts to make drawing boundaries around it difficult. Reaching conclusions about methods or effects that apply broadly across an ever more diverse field is daunting.

Yet such a stocktaking, imperfect though it will inevitably be, is necessary. Since the late 1980s, democracy aid has evolved from a specialized niche into a substantial, well-institutionalized domain that affects political developments in almost every corner of the globe. A quarter-century ago, the field was thinly populated, principally by the institutes affiliated with each of the major German and US political parties, the US National Endowment for Democracy (NED), the Latin America Bureau of the US Agency for International Development (USAID), the International Foundation for Election Systems, and a few other organizations. Today, nearly every Western government gives some aid for democracy-building, whether through its foreign ministry, bilateral-aid agency, or other institutions.

Likewise, the family of political-party foundations and multiparty institutes that offer political aid across borders has expanded greatly. Numerous private US and European foundations now fund programs to foster greater political openness and pluralism. An ever-growing range of transnational NGOs, both nonprofit "mission-driven" organizations and for-profit consulting firms, carry out programs aimed at strengthening democratic processes and institutions. Many multilateral organizations have entered the field as well. These include the UN Development Programme, the UN Democracy Fund, the International Institute for Democracy and Electoral Assistance, and regional organizations such as the Organization for Security and Co-operation in Europe and the Organization of American States. Moreover, the governments of some of the larger "emerging democracies," such as Brazil, India, Indonesia, and Turkey, are starting to use aid to support democratic change in their own respective neighborhoods.

With this striking growth in the number of actors has come a similar swelling of resources. In the late 1980s, less than US $1 billion a year went to democracy assistance. Today, the total is more than $10 billion. This spending translates into thousands of projects that directly engage hundreds of thousands of people in the developing and postcommunist worlds. The expansion of democracy aid also entails a widening reach. Two and a half decades ago, most democracy aid flowed to Latin America and a few Asian countries, such as the Philippines and Taiwan. In the intervening years, it has spread around the world, following the democratic wave as it washed across Central and Eastern Europe, the former Soviet Union, sub-Saharan Africa, the Balkans, Asia, and the Middle

East. Today, at least some democracy aid reaches every country that has moved away from authoritarian rule, as well as most countries still living under dictatorship. When new political transitions look promising, as they did in Burma and Tunisia several years back, a scramble occurs as organizations trip over one another in search of ways to bring democracy aid to bear.

Despite this impressive growth, many practitioners and observers wonder whether the field is adopting smarter methods over time and achieving better results or just repeating itself in an endless loop of set approaches and inflated but never-fulfilled expectations. These lingering doubts come at a time when democracy aid is becoming increasingly controversial, a target for power holders in many parts of the world who attack it as a form of subversion that deserves to be met with harsh countermeasures. Democracy's travails in many countries where it has long held sway, plus the waning of the optimism that accompanied the spread of democracy when the "third wave" was at its height, fuel serious questioning in diverse quarters about whether democracy support is even a legitimate enterprise. In short, as democracy aid reaches the quarter-century mark it remains far short of the settled, comfortable state of maturity that many of its early adherents expected (or at least hoped) it would be able to claim after decades of effort. Instead, it is beset by deep uncertainties about how far it has come and about the way forward.

A PATTERN OF LEARNING

In its early years, democracy aid rapidly took shape around a three-part framework consisting of (1) support for institutions and processes crucial to democratic contestation—above all, free and fair elections and political-party development; (2) the strengthening and reform of key state institutions, especially those checking the power of centralized executives, such as parliaments, judiciaries, and local governments; and (3) support for civil society, usually in the form of help offered to public-interest NGOs, independent media outlets, labor unions, and civic-education initiatives. Today, if one goes to a country that is moving away from authoritarian rule and surveys the democracy-aid programs under way there, most will fit within this framework. In short, democracy aid—in outline at least—continues to look much as it did back in the late 1980s. The three main types on offer then are still the three main types on offer. Look a little deeper, however, and changes become apparent. Broadly speaking, the changes reflect a pattern of learning from experience.

Studying each of the main lines of democracy-aid programming, one sees at least partial evolution away from the glaring shortcomings that often bedeviled early democracy-aid efforts. These shortcomings included attempting to export Western institutional models, failing to grasp local contexts in any depth, and naively assuming that positive postauthoritarian dynamics would somehow sweep aside all resistance to democratic change. At least some parts of the democracy-aid community have overcome these and other weaknesses as regards methods. They are seeking to facilitate locally generated and rooted forms of change, analyzing the terrain thoroughly before acting, and taking seriously the challenge of identifying and nurturing domestic drivers of change that can overcome entrenched resistance to democratizing reforms. Such changes have improved work in most of the major areas of democracy aid, such as (to give a partial list) election monitoring, civil society development, and rule-of-law building.

Early on, international election observation was too often a hasty fly-in, fly-out affair, long on publicity and short on depth. Today, at least the more serious groups engaged in such work understand that effective election monitoring requires establishing a long-term in-country presence and assessing the electoral process in its entirety, not just on voting day. Observers from such groups now more frequently support and partner with capable domestic monitoring groups. Rather than merely rendering simple "thumbs-up" or "thumbs-down" judgments, their assessment reports attempt to convey the complexity of electoral processes. And these groups are more apt than before to weigh whether sending a monitoring mission risks allowing clever antidemocratic power holders to exploit its presence to legitimate their artful electoral deceits.

At least some civil society development work has evolved beyond the romanticism and superficiality that marked much of this kind of aid in the 1990s. Back then, elite advocacy groups tended to attract the most donor support, even when they lacked sufficient rootedness, local legitimacy, and sustainability. Today, some aid organizations do things differently. They are emphasizing the need for local civil society to focus on constituency building, striving to reach groups beyond the narrow range of Westernized donor favorites, giving local groups means and incentives to find their own local sources of support, and working to ensure that outside aid spurs cooperation rather than infighting within the local civil society scene.

In the rule-of-law domain, the early narrow, top-down interpretation of rule-of-law development as primarily a question of training judges, prosecutors, and police officers has given way to broader perspectives, which include programs to strengthen legal education, improve legal access for the poor, advance legal empowerment, and strengthen civic organizations that exert pressure on the state's reform-resistant legal institutions. In addition, some aid groups have moved beyond the traditional focus on the formal legal sphere to work with customary or traditional institutions that are involved in resolving disputes and administering justice more generally.

Similar patterns of learning from experience can be seen in the other main areas of democracy support. In addition, democracy-aid strategies have become more country-specific. Decades ago, such strategic differentiation was rare. Assuming that transitions toward democracy would unfold in much the same way across diverse countries, aid providers favored a standard menu that entailed distributing aid somewhat evenly across all the types of programming included in the three-part framework.

This approach, however, soon showed its flaws. The growing heterogeneity of political paths among those countries striving to leave authoritarianism behind obliged providers of democracy aid to think about strategies more carefully and develop a wider array of them. For countries whose exit from authoritarian rule has led them only to semiauthoritarian stasis, for instance, the standard menu is clearly inadequate. Realizing that in this kind of setting a focus on institutions such as electoral commissions, parliaments, and judiciaries is likely to be of scant value, democracy-aid providers worth their strategic salt will concentrate instead on trying to keep some independent civil society and media organs alive. In a semiauthoritarian country with a dynamic, growing economy, democracy support may work for greater pluralism and a fuller rule of law by backing the efforts of independent business people who want fairer, more transparent rules and a greater say in major political decisions.

The standard menu is also inadequate in countries that have exited authoritarianism only to end up cycling in and out of civil conflict. Aid providers may instead try to concentrate on activities such as bridge-building among contending groups, constitutional reform, security-sector reform, and support for those parts of civil society actively contributing to reconciliation efforts. Still other countries have become stuck in shallow forms of democracy where there is some formal alternation of power but where elites remain so deeply entrenched that the turnover is mainly a matter of offices changing hands within unchanging circles while most citizens' concerns go ignored. In such places, the smartest democracy support tries to look beyond conventional programming. The search instead is for ways to encourage new entrants into the stagnant political-party scene, to help citizens convert their anger at corruption and disempowerment into serious pressure for reform, to create positive links between socioeconomic advocacy campaigns and political reforms, and to assist social movements that reach a wide base.

Another area of positive evolution based on learning from experience involves the growing relationship between democracy assistance and other parts of the international-aid domain, above all, the dominant area of socioeconomic aid. The first generation of democracy-aid practitioners often wanted to stay apart from the world of socioeconomic aid. Their mission, they felt, was fundamentally different—not poverty reduction or economic growth, but political transformation. They were wary of traditional aid providers' willingness often to work cooperatively with corrupt, repressive governments and were put off by what they perceived as the rigid, bureaucratized structures of socioeconomic aid. Traditional aid providers, meanwhile, returned the favor: they feared that allowing socioeconomic assistance to become linked to explicitly political activities would damage their relations with aid-receiving governments. Some were also put off by what they saw as the improvised, even "cowboy" methods of democracy promoters who were suddenly racing around the world talking about bringing large-scale changes to countries they seemed scarcely to know.

Hesitantly at first, but more concertedly over the past ten years, practitioners on both sides of the aid divide have taken steps to narrow it and to create positive synergies between the two domains. Increasingly faced with the threat that poor socioeconomic performance poses to fledgling democratic transitions, some democracy promoters are actively exploring how strengthening democracy can more directly advance socioeconomic progress. At the same time, many developmentalists have embraced the idea that political pathologies, such as systematic corruption and excessive power concentrations, create basic problems for socioeconomic development. At first, this embrace gave rise to governance programs that focused in mainly technocratic ways on efficiency and capability. But over time, socioeconomic-aid providers have broadened their view to take on relations between power holders and citizens, emphasizing relational concepts such as accountability, transparency, participation, and inclusion. In addition, the rising focus on governance has led some socioeconomic-aid providers to work closely with institutions that democracy aid has long worked with, such as judiciaries, parliaments, and local councils.

CONTINUED SHORTCOMINGS

The positive evolution of democracy aid based on learning from experience is an important trend, but sadly it is still only a partial and inconsistent one. Alongside the progress that one can find in each of the main lines of democracy programming, one also still encounters aid efforts that are seemingly untouched by learning and rely on weak methods from decades past. In election monitoring, for example, some organizations exhibit bad habits such as failures of objectivity and lack of attention to the risk of legitimating flawed elections. A recent European Stability Initiative report highlighting serious deficiencies in the election-monitoring work that the European Parliament and the Parliamentary Assembly of the Council of Europe have done in Azerbaijan makes discouraging reading.[1]

Some funders of civil society development still channel most of their aid to a limited circle of favored NGOs in the capital city, organizations that carry out technocratic advocacy efforts based on externally determined agendas. In the rule-of-law area, some aid providers have failed to move beyond stale judicial-strengthening efforts that rely on rote best-practices training while ignoring the broader array of entrenched obstacles that prevent ordinary citizens from achieving justice.[2]

The picture is similarly mixed with regard to the diversification of strategies. Some groups engaged in democracy work, especially the smaller ones that focus exclusively on it, are trying hard to think strategically and to move beyond the standard menu of approaches. Yet others, especially some of the larger organizations for which democracy work is only a small part of their overall portfolio, still sometimes operate on strategic autopilot, carrying out many types of programs in any one setting with little careful thought about which among them offer the most fruitful avenues for change. These autopilot approaches not only produce poorly conceived programs that fail to pinpoint key issues in troubled transitions but also undercut the efforts of those actors that are trying to be more strategic. For example, some aid groups may attempt to pursue rule-of-law change in a thoughtful way, working with citizens' groups pushing for change and avoiding official institutions dominated by those benefiting from the system as it is. Yet other aid providers may then come in to swath the official institutions in blankets of loans or technical assistance that effectively insulate these institutions against the efforts of those pushing from below.

With regard to bridging the gap between democracy aid and the larger, older domain of socioeconomic aid, the glass is similarly only half full. Even as they admit the need to give more attention to politics in their work, many mainstream developmentalists remain opposed to broadening their definition of development to include democratic norms. Sweden remains alone among major donor countries in embracing Amartya Sen's notion of "development as freedom." Most still treat democracy as, at best, a pleasing "extra." Some even see it as a negative factor that more often complicates socioeconomic development than facilitates it. Although the majority of large aid providers devote at least some funding to democracy programming, often under the less political-sounding label of "aid for democratic governance," they have been slow to integrate the principles and practices of such work into their main areas of activity, consigning democracy work to the margins of their own institutional structures.

In short, learning from experience in democracy aid has been real and significant but less consistent and far-reaching than we might hope. The reasons for this are no mystery. Accumulating and acting on knowledge drawn from experience is a chronic problem for international assistance generally. Aid providers do carry out many program evaluations. But they are deeply wary of outside critical scrutiny and too rarely fund the sort of in-depth, independent studies that examine the underlying assumptions, methods, and outcomes in a sector of democracy aid.

The intensified focus on monitoring and evaluation that has gripped the aid world in recent years has not helped. Many monitoring and evaluation efforts are too narrow to shed much light on the larger questions that one must answer in order to craft effective democracy aid. What factors, for instance, are crucial to the emergence of the rule of law? How can parties overcome deep public alienation from anything that smacks of politics? How can civil society activism lead to organized efforts to build political institutions? As democracy-aid practitioners well know, the heightened attention to monitoring and evaluation often produces artificial and reductionist program indicators, rigid implementation frameworks, and unrealistic goals—all things that work directly against key lessons from experience about the need for flexible, adaptive programming.

Beyond lack of investment in deep-reaching qualitative research and resistance to critical outside scrutiny lie problems arising from the basic political economy of the aid industry. Many aid organizations are designed and operate more for the interests of aid providers than recipients. They impose agendas from the top down rather than allowing them to percolate from the bottom up. They obsess over risk reduction and central control, choking off innovation and flexibility in the process. They cling to standard project methods that unhelpfully frontload project design, insist on unrealistically short time frames for achieving change, and favor imported Western expertise over the local variety. Moreover, as the democracy-aid domain has grown and aged, it has become subject to what Sarah Bush has usefully warned about as "the taming of democracy assistance"—the tendency of some democracy-aid providers to become more concerned over time with maintaining their budgets and their "market share" in other countries by carrying out soft, unchallenging programs and avoiding incisive, challenging efforts to advance change.[3]

TURBULENT WATERS

If we look just at the enterprise of democracy aid itself, we see an assistance domain that is growing considerably in size and reach and absorbing some valuable lessons, albeit more slowly and partially than one might wish. Yet a wider focus is essential: The international context in which this enterprise operates has changed tremendously, especially in the past ten years. Democracy aid has entered murky, troubled waters, creating fundamental challenges for it.

When democracy aid came of age in the 1990s, an interlocking set of positive assumptions about the place of democracy and democracy aid in the world prevailed. It was assumed that

- democracy was spreading globally,
- doors were opening to democracy aid in many parts of the world,
- Western liberal democracy commanded respect and admiration globally and neither had nor was likely to have any strong ideological rivals, and
- the weight of democracy as a foreign-policy priority of established Western democracies was increasing and would continue to increase.

Over the past decade, a cascade of negative developments has called into question or even toppled each of these rosy assumptions. Democracy practitioners confront a daunting set of harsh new realities. These include:

1. *A loss of democratic momentum.* The global stagnation of democracy is one of the most significant international political developments of the past decade. Democracy's failure to keep expanding has hurt the democratic-assistance field in at least two ways. First, it has sapped energy and impetus. Democracy-aid providers know that tough cases in which transitions are blocked or never really get under way are facts of life. What compensates for them are the promising cases—the times and places where democracy does break through and gain a foothold. These exciting opportunities are crucial. They make other parts of the policy community take notice,

and indeed give life and force to the whole democracy-assistance enterprise.

Over the past ten years, the flow of such good news has slowed to a trickle. Stories about how the democratic spirit is manifesting itself in this or that surprising place have been cast into shadow by persistent democratic deficiencies or backsliding in Afghanistan, Hungary, Iraq, Mali, Russia, Sri Lanka, Thailand, and many other places. For a short time in 2011, the "Arab Spring" looked as if it might be the start of a new global democratic wave, but that initial burst of hope has given way to pessimism. Now, many Western policy makers and analysts are asking whether efforts to foster democracy in the Arab world even make sense given the instability and conflict that political change has brought. With the democratic cause stalled (or even losing ground) around the world, democracy-aid providers must battle a growing sense in the Western policy community that the historical moment for democracy aid has passed.

Furthermore, the loss of democratic momentum raises questions in the wider policy community about the impact of democracy aid. The welter of factors that affect transitions makes it problematic to assess the effect of such aid based just on democracy's macro-level progress. Yet when democracy is on the rise in many places, democracy aid almost inevitably gains credibility by association. And when democracy is faring poorly in the world, hard questions about the effectiveness of democracy assistance are asked. Some recent or ongoing cases offer sobering examples of the limits of democracy aid:

- In Russia, long-term benefits from the wide range of Western democracy programs that got under way in the 1990s and operated into the last decade—including rule-of-law aid, electoral aid, political-party building, work with independent media, and support for civil society—may not be entirely absent, but they are certainly limited at best.

- For years, Western aid providers held up Mali as one of Africa's democratic success stories. Yet the vertiginous collapse of the

Malian government in 2012 underlined how hollow even apparent success stories of democracy support can be.

- The United States and others have provided substantial rule-of-law aid to El Salvador for 30 years. Despite this, El Salvador today is notoriously beset by shockingly high crime levels that have overwhelmed its criminal-justice system.

Moreover, the fact that some of the largest investments in democracy assistance have been made in such difficult locales as Afghanistan and Iraq, with deeply problematic results, has contributed to the questioning of its impact.

2. *Closing of doors.* When some governments that had previously allowed in significant amounts of prodemocracy aid began pushing back against it in the early 2000s, observers thought this might be a short-term phenomenon. The George W. Bush administration's emphasis on democracy promotion in its intervention in Iraq, along with Western support for some of the civic groups that were active in the "color revolutions" in Georgia, Kyrgyzstan, and Ukraine, had triggered heightened sensitivities about democracy aid in various places, especially Russia and other post-Soviet countries. But even as the color revolutions faded into the past and a new US president took a far less assertive stance on democracy promotion, the backlash kept growing.

In just the past few years, dozens of governments, in every region of the world, have been taking a medley of formal and informal measures to block, limit, or stigmatize international aid for democracy and human rights, especially civil society support, political-party work, and election monitoring. Aid from the United States is sometimes the principal target, as in 2013 when the Bolivian government charged that USAID was meddling in politics and ordered it to leave the country. Yet the backlash is hitting other providers as well: To cite just one of many examples, the Hungarian government recently began harassing Hungarian civil society organizations for their acceptance of Norwegian government funding.

Pushback—which is often strongest in countries where democratization is in trouble and outside assistance is most badly needed—has multiple negative effects. Most obviously, it often prevents democracy-aid providers from operating. Central Asian governments, for instance, decided about a decade ago to limit externally sponsored aid for civil society development, and looking around the region today one sees a greatly reduced pool of such aid. Restrictive measures by Egypt and some other Arab countries have similarly reduced outside support for nongovernmental organizations in their territories.

Even when pushback does not reduce the amount of democracy aid that reaches a country, it may end up changing the type of democracy support that is offered. To avoid problems, democracy promoters may hold back from politically challenging types of assistance, such as aid for independent human-rights groups or media organizations, and limit themselves to soft-focus governance programming. Similarly, pushback may cause some activist groups receiving democracy aid from abroad to avoid activities that they fear their governments may find too challenging.

3. *The troubles of Western democracies.* The struggle of Western liberal democracy to maintain the unrivaled pride of place that it enjoyed in the 1990s also affects democracy aid. Democracy's travails in both the United States and Europe have greatly damaged the standing of democracy in the eyes of many people around the world. In the United States, dysfunctional political polarization, the surging role of money in politics, and distortions in representation due to gerrymandering are particular problems. In Europe, the euro crisis, the rise of extremist parties, and challenges surrounding the social integration of minority communities are raising doubts about democracy's health. At the same time, the growing self-confidence and assertiveness of other political systems, especially authoritarian or semiauthoritarian regimes in China, Russia, Turkey, Ethiopia, and elsewhere, are making some people in transitional countries wonder whether the keys to decisive governance and economic

dynamism do not in fact lie down some path other than that of liberal democracy.

These developments inevitably weaken Western democracy-aid efforts. A US group going abroad to offer advice and training on how to strengthen a country's parliament will face punishing questions about the credibility of its offerings given the manifest deficiencies and unpopularity of the US Congress. The same will be true for a European group seeking to help another country bridge a sectarian divide based on religious differences. Of course, smart democracy assistance does not seek to export a particular national model but instead offers insights gleaned from comparative experiences and tries to help locals craft their own solutions. Nevertheless, all Western democracy promoters must work harder than before to establish their credibility in other parts of the world, and in some quarters (e.g., East Asia) they sometimes barely receive a hearing. Moreover, they can no longer assume that their task is to help local actors move ahead with democracy. Instead, they now often face the harder, more fundamental task of convincing locals that democracy is preferable to other systems.

Furthermore, Western democracy promoters are increasingly finding their efforts challenged and sometimes undercut by nondemocratic powers intent on influencing the political trajectories of other countries. A Western-sponsored anticorruption program in an African country may be outweighed by the deleterious effects on governance of a Chinese economic-aid package that creates perverse political-economy incentives. A program to help create a level playing field among political parties in an Arab country may be undermined by large streams of Iranian or Gulf money flowing to one of them. An undertaking to support free and fair elections in a Latin American country may be distorted by Venezuela's engagement aimed at tilting the elections toward a preferred candidate.

Russia, China, Iran, the United Arab Emirates, Saudi Arabia, Venezuela, Qatar, Rwanda, Ethiopia, and other nondemocratic countries seeking heightened influence in the political life of their neighbors (or further afield) are not always bent on checking the influence of Western democracy-promotion efforts. And their actions are not necessarily aimed at promoting autocracy per se. But often they do cut against Western democracy aid and push other countries in an antidemocratic direction. Western democracy aid, having come of age at a time when it was often the dominant external form of political influence in most transitions, is now facing a markedly harsher, more competitive environment.

4. *A feebler policy commitment.* Of course, not all aspects of the international environment are unfavorable for democracy work. New communications technologies are helping prodemocratic networks to expand across borders and oceans and bringing political abuses to light. Repeated efforts by determined, courageous citizens in different parts of the world to protest against political wrongs are inspirational and underline the urgency of helping such people to translate their energies into sustained political gains. Yet the headwinds buffeting democracy aid—the waning of global democratic momentum, the growing pushback against democracy aid, the damaged status of Western democracy, and rising competition from nondemocracies—also influence many Western policy makers and add up to a further challenge: weakened commitment by the United States and other established democracies to making democracy support a foreign-policy priority.

In the 1990s, democracy promotion was clearly on the rise in Western foreign policy. As democracy expanded across the globe, it looked to Western politicians like a "growth stock" worth significant investment. Countervailing policy interests, such as the need to maintain strong ties with oil-rich authoritarian regimes, while certainly still present, appeared to be in decline. Democracy support appealed as a way to give definition to the optimistic spirit of the era and to provide an overarching policy framework at a time of post–Cold War policy drift. Although both US presidents Bill Clinton and George W. Bush and some of their counterparts in other Western democracies pursued democracy-related policies that were marred by compromises and contradictions, they did try to find a place for it near the center of their foreign-policy visions.

That outlook no longer holds. With democracy stagnant or in retreat in many parts of the world, Western politicians have less incentive to associate themselves with the cause. Democratization has come to appear to many Western policy makers as a risky, even ill-advised endeavor in some places due to its potential for unleashing sectarian conflict, as in Iraq and Libya, or for giving rise to populist, anti-Western politicians, as in Hungary and various parts of Latin America. Moreover, as more developing countries make big new oil and gas finds or become front-line states in counterterrorism struggles, the number of countries where the West feels a tangible need to befriend nondemocratic governments is increasing.

The result is a highly uncertain commitment on the part of the Obama administration and some of its allies to put democracy high on their foreign-policy agendas. Although some advisors around President Obama insist that he is strongly committed to democracy promotion, contrary evidence is more persuasive and shows a US hesitation to push hard for democratization in many places. As the century's second decade nears its midpoint, the United States and Europe are preoccupied with daunting security challenges in the Middle East, the former Soviet Union, and East Asia that many policy makers read as making political stability rather than democratic change the overriding priority.

Thus, even though the overall spending worldwide on democracy aid is generally holding steady (despite drops at some major institutions such as USAID, where spending on democracy programs has shrunk significantly over the past five years), the aid is less grounded in policy frameworks that support the overall endeavor of advancing democracy. So if a government cracks down on civil society aid from abroad, the diplomatic response from the affected Western governments may be weak, as it was when Egypt took harsh steps in this direction in 2012 and 2013. Or an international election-monitoring effort may find serious shortcomings in an electoral process, but result in no negative consequences for the regime because the Western governments sponsoring the effort are fearful of offending a useful friend, as was recently the case with Azerbaijan. In other words, the "low policy" of democracy support remains in place, but it often cannot count on the "high-policy" side for backing when it matters.

A BASIC CHOICE

A quarter-century into its existence, the enterprise of assisting democracy across borders finds itself in an unusually complex state. On the one hand, it has grown in size and evolved positively in response to learning from experience. Yet now it must endure and make gains in a harsher international context, marked by an array of crosscurrents that have come on very strongly in the last several years, radically eroding the structural underpinnings that helped democracy aid to flourish in the 1990s.

The democracy-aid community is only just starting to come to terms with this much more troubled context. The major difficulties posed by this environment will not go away anytime soon. Democracy-aid providers need to invest much more energy and resources in finding ways to adapt and respond. With regard to the closing-space problem, signs of a strengthening response are emerging. Some of the most heavily affected aid providers, such as the US government, are working on a menu of measures that includes strengthening the international norms protecting civil society's freedoms, better coordinating diplomatic campaigns against restrictive NGO laws, and providing protective technologies to local partners threatened with surveillance and harassment. There is no magic bullet that will vanquish the closing-space phenomenon. A great deal more will need to be done, and by a wide range of aid actors, but at least a start has been made.

In contrast, democracy-aid providers have shown less willingness to confront the problems of Western democracy's declining prestige and the growing competition from alternative political models. Some Western aid practitioners still talk behind closed doors about the special value of their own country's political system and their mission of bringing its benefits to distant lands. They seem startlingly unaware of just how damaged Western models have become in the eyes of others and how much democracy aid needs to be built on far more modest assumptions about the relative appeal of Western democracy. A few groups, including the US-based National Democratic Institute, have for some time emphasized comparative expertise drawn from established and transitional countries alike and hired many non-Western staffers with experience from other transitions, but such practices are still too rare in the aid community. In addition, aid providers need to go beyond their ritualistic assertions of openness to democratic variety, working together in a more focused way with those in other parts of the world who insist on a preference for non-Western forms of democracy, in order to clarify whether such alternatives are compatible with core universal principles of democracy and how Western democracy aid can support more varied but still legitimate democratic approaches.[4]

Regarding the diminishing Western commitment to making democracy support a foreign-policy priority, democracy-aid providers can play a counterbalancing role by drawing on their experiences around the world to address more systematically the growing concerns of Western policy makers about democracy. How can Western governments insert an effective prodemocracy element into their dealings with democratically deficient but strategically useful governments without sacrificing a broader cooperative relationship with them? Why should flawed democratic development be regarded not just as a side issue in many of the security threats that are flaring up from Ukraine to Iraq, but as a root cause of them? How can elections be designed and supported in ways that specifically help to reduce the chance of emergent sectarian conflicts? By answering questions such as these, the "low-policy" side of democracy support (that is, democracy aid) can move away from its tendency to view itself merely as a beneficiary (or victim) of the "high-policy" side of democracy support and take on a significant role in shaping it instead.

The forbidding waters in which democracy aid now finds itself are prompting quiet but audible talk of a fundamental crisis facing the field. This talk is mistaken. The context is indeed daunting, yet this is not especially surprising. For too long democracy promoters have tried to hold on to the appealing but incorrect idea that rapidly expanding democracy, opening doors, and a lack of ideological rivals are natural global conditions that will continue indefinitely. In other words, democracy aid is not facing an existential crisis so much as it is coming up against hard realities that are far from historically unusual when seen in a longer-term perspective. For the foreseeable future, democracy aid will have to operate principally in countries rife with forbidding obstacles to democratization; power holders in many places will resist and resent such aid; and alternative political models will vie hard for attention and influence. Coming to terms with these realities is not about dealing with crisis, but rather about shedding lingering illusions.

In short, democracy aid has arrived not at a crisis, but at a crossroads, defined by two very different possible paths forward. Some democracy-aid providers facing the new environment will feel inclined to pull back, spend fewer resources, exit from difficult countries, trim their political sails, and avoid direct competition with contending models. In short, they will aim to reduce their risks and their ambitions. Others will favor a different path. They will accept that backsliding, closing political space, and greater competition are the "new normal" of democracy aid. They will invest more heavily in learning, accept the need to tolerate greater risks, work harder to achieve greater cooperation and solidarity among diverse democracy-aid providers, and argue more effectively for principled, persuasive prodemocracy diplomacy to support their efforts.

It is unclear which of these paths will attract more adherents among the large set of relevant actors. But the eventual answer to this question will do much to determine whether a stocktaking of democracy aid another quarter-century down the road will tell a story of decline and growing irrelevance or reveal a pattern of sustained productive engagement and iterative progress in the face of significant adversity.

NOTES

The author thanks Ken Wollack and Richard Youngs for helpful comments on a draft and Mahroh Jahangiri and Oren Samet-Marram for research assistance.

1. European Stability Initiative, "Disgraced: Azerbaijan and the End of Election Monitoring as We Know It," 5 November 2013, available at *www.esiweb.org.*
2. David Marshall, ed., *The International Rule of Law Movement: A Crisis of Legitimacy and the Way Forward* (Cambridge: Harvard University Press, 2014).
3. Sarah Bush, *The Taming of Democracy Assistance: Why Democracy Promotion Does Not Confront Dictators* (Cambridge: Cambridge University Press, 2015).
4. Richard Youngs of the Carnegie Endowment's Democracy and Rule of Law Program has been examining the rise of calls for non-Western democracy and their implications for Western democracy aid. He asks whether those calling for non-Western forms of democracy are simply seeking rhetorical camouflage for nondemocratic approaches and to what extent genuine variety is possible without sacrificing the core principles without which liberal democracy cannot exist. The Carnegie Endowment will publish his findings in book form in 2015.

6

Facing Up to the Democratic Recession

LARRY DIAMOND

The year 2014 marked the fortieth anniversary of Portugal's Revolution of the Carnations, which inaugurated what Samuel P. Huntington dubbed the "third wave" of global democratization. Any assessment of the state of global democracy today must begin by recognizing—even marveling at—the durability of this historic transformation. When the third wave began in 1974, only about 30 percent of the world's independent states met the criteria of electoral democracy—a system in which citizens, through universal suffrage, can choose and replace their leaders in regular, free, fair, and meaningful elections.[1] At that time, there were only about 46 democracies in the world. Most of those were the liberal democracies of the rich West, along with a number of small island states that had been British colonies. Only a few other developing democracies existed—principally, India, Sri Lanka, Costa Rica, Colombia, Venezuela, Israel, and Turkey.

In the subsequent three decades, democracy had a remarkable

global run, as the number of democracies essentially held steady or expanded every year from 1975 until 2007. Nothing like this continuous growth in democracy had ever been seen before in the history of the world. While a number of these new "democracies" were quite illiberal—in some cases, so much so that Steven Levitsky and Lucan Way regard them as "competitive authoritarian" regimes[2]—the positive three-decade trend was paralleled by a similarly steady and significant expansion in levels of freedom (political rights and civil liberties, as measured annually by Freedom House). In 1974, the average level of freedom in the world stood at 4.38 (on the two 7-point scales, where 1 is most free and 7 is most repressive). It then gradually improved during the 1970s and 1980s, though it did not cross below the 4.0 midpoint until the fall of the Berlin Wall, after which it improved to 3.85 in 1990. In 25 of the 32 years between 1974 and 2005, average freedom levels improved in the world, peaking at 3.22 in 2005.

And then, around 2006, the expansion of freedom and democracy in the world came to a prolonged halt. Since 2006, there has been no net expansion in the number of electoral democracies, which has oscillated between 114 and 119 (about 60 percent of the world's states). As we see in figure 1, the number of both electoral and liberal democracies began to decline after 2006 and then flattened out.[3] Since 2006, the average level of freedom in the world has also deteriorated slightly, leveling off at about 3.30.

There are two ways to view these empirical trends. One is to see them as constituting a period of equilibrium—freedom and democracy have not continued gaining, but neither have they experienced net declines. One could even celebrate this as an expression of the remarkable and unexpected durability of the democratic wave. Given that democracy expanded to a number of countries where the objective conditions for sustaining it are unfavorable, due either to poverty (for example, in Liberia, Malawi, and Sierra Leone) or to strategic pressures (for example, in Georgia and Mongolia), it is impressive that reasonably open and competitive political systems have survived (or revived) in so many places. As a variant of this more benign interpretation, Levitsky and Way argue in Chapter Four of this volume that democracy never actually expanded as widely as Freedom House perceived in the first place. Thus, they contend, many of the seeming failures of democracy in the last ten to fifteen years were really deteriorations or hardenings of what had been from the beginning authoritarian regimes, however competitive.

Alternatively, one can view the last decade as a period of at least incipient decline in democracy. To make this case, we need to examine not only the instability and stagnation of democracies but also the incremental decline of democracy in what Thomas Carothers has termed the "gray zone" countries (which defy easy classification as to whether or not they are democracies),[4] the deepening authoritarianism in the nondemocracies, and the decline in the functioning and self-confidence of the world's established, rich democracies. This will be my approach in what follows.

The debate about whether there has been a decline in democracy turns to some extent on how we count it. It is one of the great and probably inescapable ironies of scholarly research that the boom in comparative democratic studies has been accompanied by significant disagreement over how to define and measure democracy. I have never felt that there was—or could be—one right and consensual answer to this eternal conceptual challenge. Most scholars of democracy have agreed that it makes sense to classify regimes categorically—and thus to determine which regimes are democracies and which are not. But democracy is in many ways a continuous variable. Its key components—such as freedom of multiple parties and candidates to campaign and contest, opposition access to mass media and campaign finance, inclusiveness of suffrage, fairness and neutrality of electoral administration, and the extent to which electoral victors have meaningful power to rule—vary on a continuum (as do other dimensions of the quality of democracy, such as civil liberties, rule of law, control of corruption, vigor of civil society, and so on). This continuous variation forces coders to make difficult judgments about how to classify regimes that fall into the gray zone of ambiguity, where multiparty electoral competition is genuine and vigorous but flawed in some notable ways. No system of multiparty competition is perfectly fair and open. Some multiparty electoral systems clearly do not meet the test of democracy. Others have serious defects that nevertheless do not negate their overall democratic character. Thus hard decisions must often be made about how to weight imperfections and where to draw the line.

FIGURE 1. The growth of democracies in the world, 1974–2013

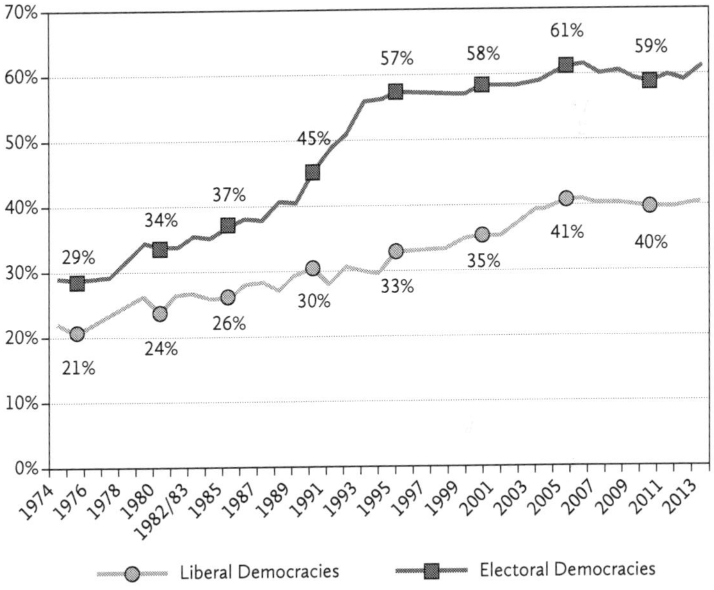

Most approaches to classifying regimes (as democracies or not) rely on continuous measurement of key variables (such as political rights, in the case of the Polity scale, or both political rights and civil liberties, in the case of Freedom House), along with a somewhat arbitrary cutoff point for separating democracies from nondemocracies.[5] My own method has been to accept the Freedom House coding decisions except where I find persuasive contradictory evidence. This has led to my counting two to five fewer democracies than Freedom House does for most years since 1989; for some years, the discrepancy is much larger.[6]

THE DEMOCRATIC RECESSION: BREAKDOWNS AND EROSIONS

The world has been in a mild but protracted democratic recession since about 2006. Beyond the lack of improvement or modest erosion of global levels of democracy and freedom, there have been several other causes for concern. First, there has been a significant and, in fact, accelerating rate of democratic breakdown. Second, the quality or stability of democracy has been declining in a number of large and strategically important emerging-market countries, which I call "swing states." Third, authoritarianism has been deepening, including in big and strategically important countries. And fourth, the established democracies, beginning with the United States, increasingly seem to be performing poorly and to lack the will and self-confidence to promote democracy effectively abroad. I explore each of these in turn.

First, let us look at rates of democratic breakdown. Between 1974 and the end of 2014, 29 percent of all the democracies in the world broke down (among non-Western democracies, the rate was 35 percent). In the first decade and a half of this new century, the failure rate (17.6 percent) has been substantially higher than in the preceding fifteen-year period (12.7 percent). Alternatively, if we break the third wave up into its four component decades, we see a rising incidence of democratic failure per decade since the mid-1980s. The rate of democratic failure, which had been 16 percent in the first decade of the third wave (1974–83), fell to 8 percent in the second decade (1984–93), but then climbed to 11 percent in the third decade (1994–2003), and most recently to 14 percent (2004–13). (If we include the three failures of 2014, the rate rises to over 16 percent.)

Since 2000, I count 25 breakdowns of democracy in the world—not only through blatant military or executive coups, but also through subtle and incremental degradations of democratic rights and procedures that finally push a democratic system over the

TABLE. Breakdowns of democracy, 2000–2014

Year of Breakdown	Country	Year of Return	Type of Breakdown
2000	Fiji	—	Military coup
2000	Russia	—	Executive degradation, violation of opposition rights
2001	Central Af. Rep.	—	Military rebellion, violence, human rights abuses
2002	Guinea-Bissau	2005	Executive degradation, violation of opposition rights (military coup the following year)
2002	Nepal	2013	Rising political instability, monarchical coup
2004	Venezuela	—	Executive degradation, violation of opposition rights
2005	Thailand	2011	Military coup, then military constraint
2006	Solomon Islands	—	Decline of democratic process
2007	Bangladesh	2008	Military "soft coup"
2007	Philippines	2010	Executive degradation
2007	Kenya	—	Electoral fraud and executive abuse
2008	Georgia	2012	Electoral fraud and executive abuse
2009	Honduras	2013	Military intervention
2009	Madagascar	—	Unconstitutional assumption of power by opposition; suspension of elected parliament
2009	Niger	2011	Presidential dissolution of Constitutional Court and National Assembly to extend presidential rule
2010	Burundi	—	Electoral fraud, opposition boycott, political closure
2010	Sri Lanka	—	Executive degradation
2010	Guinea-Bissau	—	Military intervention, weakening civilian control, deteriorating rule of law
2012	Maldives	—	Forcible removal of democratically elected president
2012	Mali	2014	Military coup
2011	Nicaragua	—	Executive degradation
2012	Ukraine	2014	Electoral fraud (parliamentary elections), executive abuse
2014	Turkey	—	Executive degradation, violation of opposition rights
2014	Bangladesh	—	Breakdown of electoral process
2014	Thailand	—	Military coup

threshold into competitive authoritarianism (see table). Some of these breakdowns occurred in quite low-quality democracies; yet in each case, a system of reasonably free and fair multiparty electoral competition was either displaced or degraded to a point well below the minimal standards of democracy.

One methodological challenge in tracking democratic breakdowns is to determine a precise date or year for a democratic failure that results from a long secular process of systemic deterioration and executive strangulation of political rights, civil liberties, and the rule of law. No serious scholar would consider Russia today a democracy. But many believe that it was an electoral democracy (however rough and illiberal) under Boris Yeltsin. If we score 1993 as the year when democracy emerged in Russia (as Freedom House does), then what year do we identify as marking the end of democracy? In this case (and many others), there is no single obvious event—like Peruvian president Alberto Fujimori's 1992 *autogolpe,* dissolving Congress and seizing unconstitutional powers—to guide the scoring decision. I postulate that Russia's political system fell below the minimum conditions of electoral democracy during the year 2000, as signaled by the electoral fraud that gave Vladimir Putin a dubious first-ballot victory and the executive degradation of political and civic pluralism that quickly followed. (Freedom House dates the failure to 2005.)

The problem has continuing and quite contemporary relevance. For a number of years now, Turkey's ruling Justice and Development Party (AKP) has been gradually eroding democratic pluralism and freedom in the country. The overall political trends have been hard to characterize, because some of the AKP's changes have made Turkey more democratic by removing the military as an autonomous veto player in politics, extending civilian control over the military, and making it harder to ban political parties that offend the "deep state" structures associated with the intensely secularist legacy of Kemal Atatürk. But the AKP has gradually entrenched its own political hegemony, extending partisan control over the judiciary and the bureaucracy, arresting journalists and intimidating dissenters in the press and academia, threatening businesses with retaliation if they fund opposition parties, and using arrests and prosecutions in cases connected to alleged coup plots to jail and remove from public life an implausibly large number of accused plotters.

This has coincided with a stunning and increasingly audacious concentration of personal power by Turkey's longtime prime minister Recep Tayyip Erdoğan, who was elected president in August 2014. The abuse and personalization of power and the constriction of competitive space and freedom in Turkey have been subtle and incremental, moving with nothing like the speed of Putin in the early 2000s. But by now, these trends appear to have crossed a threshold, pushing the country below the minimum standards of democracy. If this has happened, when did it happen? Was it in 2014, when the AKP further consolidated its hegemonic grip on power in the March local-government elections and the August presidential election? Or was it, as some liberal Turks insist, several years before, as media freedoms were visibly diminishing and an ever-wider circle of alleged coup plotters was being targeted in the highly politicized Ergenekon trials?

A similar problem exists for Botswana, where a president (Ian Khama) with a career military background evinces an intolerance of opposition and distaste for civil society beyond anything seen previously from the long-ruling Botswana Democratic Party (BDP). Increasing political violence and intimidation—including assaults on opposition politicians, the possible murder of a leading opposition candidate three months before the October 2014 parliamentary elections, and the apparent involvement of the intelligence apparatus in the bullying and coercion of the political opposition—have been moving the political system in a more authoritarian direction. Escalating pressure on the independent media, the brazen misuse of state television by the BDP, and the growing personalization and centralization of power by President Khama (as he advances his own narrow circle of family and friends while splitting the ruling party) are further signs of the deterioration, if not crisis, of democracy in Botswana.[7] Again, Levitsky and Way had argued a number of years ago that Botswana was not a genuine democracy in the first place.[8] Nevertheless, whatever kind of system it has been in recent decades, "respect for the rule of law and for established institutions and processes" began to diminish in 1998, when Khama ascended to the vice-presidency, and it has continued to decline since 2008, when the former military commander "automatically succeeded to the presidency."[9]

There are no easy and obvious answers to the conundrum of how to classify regimes in the gray zone. One can argue about whether these ambiguous regimes are still democracies—or even if they ever really were. Those who accept that a democratic breakdown has occurred can argue about when it took place. But what is beyond argument is that there is a class of regimes that in the last decade or so have experienced significant erosion in electoral fairness, political pluralism, and civic space for opposition and dissent, typically as a result of abusive executives intent upon concentrating their personal power and entrenching ruling-party hegemony. The best-known cases of this since 1999 have been Russia and Venezuela, where populist former military officer Hugo Chávez (1999–2013) gradually suffocated democratic pluralism during the first decade of this century. After Daniel Ortega returned to the presidency in Nicaragua in 2007, he borrowed many pages from Chávez's authoritarian playbook, and left-populist authoritarian presidents Evo Morales of Bolivia and Rafael Correa of Ecuador have been moving in a similar direction. In the January 2015 issue of the *Journal of Democracy*, Scott Mainwaring and Aníbal Pérez-Liñán assert that democratic erosion has occurred since 2000 in all four of these Latin American countries (Venezuela, Nicaragua, Bolivia, and Ecuador) as well as in Honduras, with Bolivia, Ecuador, and Honduras now limping along as "semidemocracies."

Of the 25 breakdowns since 2000 listed in the table, 18 occurred after 2005. Only 8 of these 25 breakdowns came as a result of military intervention (and of those 8, only 4 took the form of a conventional, blatant military coup, as happened twice in Thailand). Two other cases (Nepal and Madagascar) saw democratically elected rulers pushed out of power by other nondemocratic forces (the monarch and the political opposition, respectively). The majority of the breakdowns—thirteen—resulted from the abuse of power and the desecration of democratic institutions and practices by democratically elected rulers. Four of these took the form of widespread electoral fraud or, in the recent case of Bangladesh, a unilateral change in the rules of electoral administration (the elimination of the practice of a caretaker government before the election) that tilted the electoral playing field and triggered an opposition boycott. The other 9 failures by executive abuse involved the more gradual suffocation of democracy by democratically elected executives (though that too was occurring in several of the instances of electoral fraud, such as Ukraine under President Viktor Yanukovych [2010–14]). Overall, nearly 1 in every 5 democracies since the turn of this century has failed.

THE DECLINE OF FREEDOM AND THE RULE OF LAW

Separate and apart from democratic failure, there has also been a trend of declining freedom in a number of countries and regions since 2005. The most often cited statistic in this regard is the Freedom House finding that, in each of the eight consecutive years from 2006 through 2013, more countries declined in freedom than improved. In fact, after a post–Cold War period in which the balance was almost always highly favorable—with improvers outstripping the decliners by a ratio of two to one (or greater)—the balance simply inverted beginning in 2006. But this does not tell the whole story.

Two important elements are noteworthy, and they are both especially visible in Africa. First, the declines have tended to crystallize over time. Thus, if we compare freedom scores at the end of 2005 and the end of 2013, we see that 29 of the 49 sub-Saharan African states (almost 60 percent) declined in freedom, while only 15 (30 percent) improved and 5 remained unchanged. Moreover, 20 states in the region saw a decline in political rights, civil liberties, or both that was substantial enough to register a change on the 7-point scales (while only 11 states saw such a visible improvement). The larger states in sub-Saharan Africa (those with a population of more than 10 million) did a bit better, but not much: Freedom deteriorated in 13 of the 25 and improved in only 8.

Another problem is that the pace of decay in democratic institutions is not always evident to outside observers. In a number of countries where we take democracy for granted, such as South Africa, we should not. In fact, there is not a single country on the African continent where democracy is firmly consolidated and secure—the way it is, for example, in such third-wave democracies as South Korea, Poland, and Chile. In the global democracy-promotion community, few actors are paying attention to the growing signs of fragility in the more liberal developing democracies, not to mention the more illiberal ones.

Why have freedom and democracy been regressing in many countries? The most important and pervasive answer is, in brief, bad governance. The Freedom House measures of political rights and civil liberties both include subcategories that directly relate to the rule of law and transparency (including corruption). If we remove these subcategories from the Freedom House political-rights and civil-liberties scores and create a third distinct scale with the rule-of-law and transparency scores, the problems become more apparent. African states (like most others in the world) perform considerably worse on the rule of law and transparency than on political rights and civil liberties.[10] Moreover, rule of law and political rights have both declined perceptibly across sub-Saharan Africa since 2005, while civil liberties have oscillated somewhat more. These empirical trends are shown in figure 2, which presents the Freedom House data for these three reconfigured scales as standardized scores, ranging from 0 to 1.[11]

The biggest problem for democracy in Africa is controlling corruption and abuse of power. The decay in governance has been visible even in the best-governed African countries, such as South Africa, which suffered a steady decline in its score on rule of law and transparency (from 0.79 to 0.63) between 2005 and 2013. And as more and more African states become resource-rich with the onset

FIGURE 2. Freedom and governance trends in Africa, 2005–13

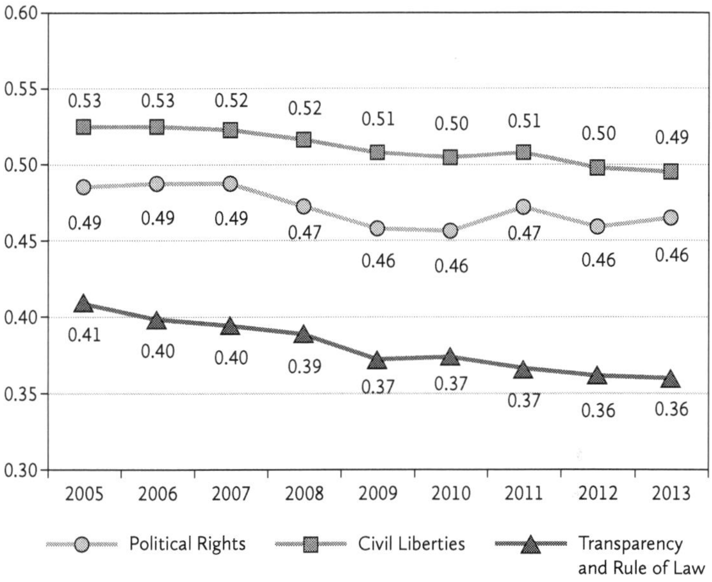

of a second African oil boom, the quality of governance will deteriorate further. This has already begun to happen in one of Africa's most liberal and important democracies, Ghana.

The problem is not unique to Africa. Every region of the world scores worse on the standardized scale of transparency and the rule of law than it does on either political rights or civil liberties. In fact, transparency and the rule of law trail the other two scales even more dramatically in Latin America, postcommunist Europe, and Asia than they do in Africa (figure 3). Many democracies in lower-income and even middle- or upper-middle-income countries (notably, Argentina) struggle with the resurgence of what Francis Fukuyama calls "neo-patrimonial" tendencies.[12] Leaders who think that they can get away with it are eroding democratic checks and balances, hollowing out institutions of accountability, overriding term limits and normative restraints, and accumulating power and wealth for themselves and their families, cronies, clients, and parties.

FIGURE 3. Political rights, civil liberties, and transparency/rule of law, 2013

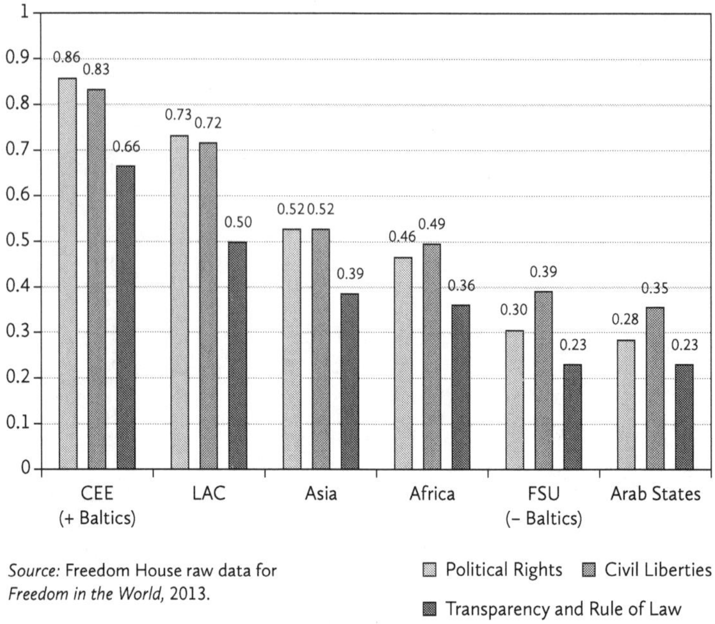

Source: Freedom House raw data for *Freedom in the World*, 2013.

In the process, they demonize, intimidate, and victimize (and occasionally even jail or murder) opponents who get in their way. Space for opposition parties, civil society, and the media is shrinking, and international support for them is drying up. Ethnic, religious, and other identity cleavages polarize many societies that lack well-designed democratic institutions to manage those cleavages. State structures are too often weak and porous—unable to secure order, protect rights, meet the most basic social needs, or rise above corrupt, clientelistic, and predatory impulses. Democratic institutions such as parties and parliaments are often poorly developed, and the bureaucracy lacks the policy expertise and, even more, the independence, neutrality, and authority to effectively manage the economy. Weak economic performance and rising inequality exacerbate the problems of abuse of power, rigging of elections, and violation of the democratic rules of the game.

THE STRATEGIC SWING STATES

A different perspective on the global state of democracy can be gleaned from a focus not on regional or global trends but on the weightiest emerging-market countries. These are the ones with large populations (say, more than 50 million) or large economies (more than US$200 billion). I count 27 of these (including Ukraine, which does not quite reach either measure but is of immense strategic importance). Twelve of these 27 swing states had worse average freedom scores at the end of 2013 than they did at the end of 2005. These declines took place across the board: in fairly liberal democracies (South Korea, Taiwan, and South Africa); in less liberal democracies (Colombia, Ukraine, Indonesia, Turkey, Mexico, and Thailand before the 2014 military coup); and in authoritarian regimes (Ethiopia, Venezuela, and Saudi Arabia). In addition, I think 3 other countries are also less free today than they were in 2005: Russia, where the noose of repressive authoritarianism has clearly been tightening since Vladimir Putin returned to the presidency in early 2012; Egypt, where the new military-dominated government under former general Abdel Fattah al-Sisi is more murderous, controlling, and intolerant than even the Mubarak regime (1981–2011); and Bangladesh, where (as noted above) democracy broke down early in 2014. Only two countries (Singapore and Pakistan) are freer today (and only modestly so) than in 2005. Some other countries have at least remained stable. Chile continues to be a liberal-democratic success story; the Philippines has returned to robust democracy after an authoritarian interlude under President Gloria Macapagal-Arroyo (2001–10); and Brazil and India have preserved robust democracy, albeit with continuing challenges. But overall, among the 27 (which also include China, Malaysia, Nigeria, and the United Arab Emirates) there has been scant evidence of democratic progress. In terms of democracy, the most important countries outside the stable democratic West have been either stagnating or slipping backward.

THE AUTHORITARIAN RESURGENCE

An important part of the story of global democratic recession has been the deepening of authoritarianism. This has taken a number of forms. In Russia, space for political opposition, principled dissent, and civil society activity outside the control of the ruling authorities has been shrinking.[13] In China, human-rights defenders and civil society activists have faced increasing harassment and victimization.

The (mainly) postcommunist autocracies of the Shanghai Cooperation Organization, centered on the axis of cynical cooperation between Russia and China, have become much more coordinated and assertive. Both countries have been aggressively flexing their muscles in dealing with their neighbors on territorial questions. And increasingly they are pushing back against democratic norms by also using instruments of soft power—international media (such as RT, Russia's slick 24/7 global television "news" channel), China's Confucius Institutes, lavish conferences, and exchange programs—to try to discredit Western democracies and democracy in general, while promoting their own models and norms.[14] This is part of a broader trend of renewed authoritarian skill and energy in using state-run media (both traditional and digital) to air an eclectic mix of pro-regime narratives, demonized images of dissenters, and illiberal, nationalist, and anti-American diatribes.[15]

African autocrats have increasingly used China's booming aid and investment (and the new regional war on Islamist terrorism) as a counterweight to Western pressure for democracy and good governance. And they have been only too happy to point to China's formula of rapid state-led development without democracy to justify their own deepening authoritarianism. In Venezuela, the vise of authoritarian populism has tightened and the government's toleration (or even organization) of criminal violence to demobilize middle-class opposition has risen. The Arab Spring has imploded in almost every country that it touched save Tunisia, leaving in most cases even more repressive states or, as in the case of Libya, hardly a state at all.

The resurgence of authoritarianism over the past eight years has been quickened by the diffusion of common tools and approaches. Prominent among these have been laws to criminalize international flows of financial and technical assistance from democracies to democratic parties, movements, media, election monitors, and civil society organizations in authoritarian regimes, as well as broader restrictions on the ability of NGOs to form and operate and the creation of pseudo-NGOs to do the bidding (domestically and internationally) of autocrats.[16] One recent study of 98 countries outside the West found that 51 of them either prohibit or restrict foreign funding of civil society, with a clear global trend toward tightening control; as a result, international democracy-assistance flows are dropping precipitously where they are needed most.[17] In addition, authoritarian (and even some democratic) states are becoming more resourceful, sophisticated, and unapologetic in suppressing Internet freedom and using cyberspace to frustrate, subvert, and control civil society.[18]

WESTERN DEMOCRACY IN RETREAT

Perhaps the most worrisome dimension of the democratic recession has been the decline of democratic efficacy, energy, and self-confidence in the West, including the United States. There is a growing sense, both domestically and internationally, that democracy in the United States has not been functioning effectively enough to address the major challenges of governance. The diminished pace of legislation, the vanishing ability of Congress to pass a budget, and the 2013 shutdown of the federal government are only some of the indications of a political system (and a broader body politic) that appears increasingly polarized and deadlocked. As a result, both public approval of Congress and public trust in government are at historic lows. The ever-mounting cost of election campaigns, the surging role of nontransparent money in politics, and low rates of voter participation are additional signs of democratic ill health. Internationally, promoting democracy abroad scores close to the bottom of the public's foreign-policy priorities.

And the international perception is that democracy promotion has already receded as an actual priority of US foreign policy.

The world takes note of all this. Authoritarian state media gleefully publicize these travails of American democracy in order to discredit democracy in general and immunize authoritarian rule against US pressure. Even in weak states, autocrats perceive that the pressure is now off: They can pretty much do whatever they want to censor the media, crush the opposition, and perpetuate their rule, and Europe and the United States will swallow it. Meek verbal protests may ensue, but the aid will still flow and the dictators will still be welcome at the White House and the Elysée Palace.

It is hard to overstate how important the vitality and self-confidence of US democracy has been to the global expansion of democracy during the third wave. While each democratizing country made its own transition, pressure and solidarity from the United State and Europe often generated a significant and even crucial enabling environment that helped to tip finely balanced situations toward democratic change, and then in some cases gradually toward democratic consolidation. If this solidarity is now greatly diminished, so will be the near-term global prospects for reviving and sustaining democratic progress.

A BRIGHTER HORIZON?

Democracy has been in a global recession for most of the last decade, and there is a growing danger that the recession could deepen and tip over into something much worse. Many more democracies could fail, not only in poor countries of marginal strategic significance, but also in big swing states such as Indonesia and Ukraine (again). There is little external recognition yet of the grim state of democracy in Turkey, and there is no guarantee that democracy will return any time soon to Thailand or Bangladesh. Apathy and inertia in Europe and the United States could significantly lower the barriers to new democratic reversals and to authoritarian entrenchments in many more states.

Yet the picture is not entirely bleak. We have not seen "a third reverse wave." Globally, average levels of freedom have ebbed a little bit, but not calamitously. Most important, there has not been significant erosion in public support for democracy. In fact, what the Afro-barometer has consistently shown is a gap—in some African countries, a chasm—between the popular demand for democracy and the supply of it provided by the regime. This is not based just on some shallow, vague notion that democracy is a good thing. Many Africans understand the importance of political accountability, transparency, the rule of law, and restraint of power, and they would like to see their governments manifest these virtues.

While the performance of democracy is failing to inspire, authoritarianism faces its own steep challenges. There is hardly a dictatorship in the world that looks stable for the long run. The only truly reliable source of regime stability is legitimacy, and the number of people in the world who believe in the intrinsic legitimacy of any form of authoritarianism is rapidly diminishing. Economic development, globalization, and the information revolution are undermining all forms of authority and empowering individuals. Values are changing, and while we should not assume any teleological path toward a global "enlightenment," generally the movement is toward greater distrust of authority and more desire for accountability, freedom, and political choice. In the coming two decades, these trends will challenge the nature of rule in China, Vietnam, Iran, and the Arab states much more than they will in India, not to mention Europe and the United States. Already, democratization is visible on the horizon of Malaysia's increasingly competitive electoral politics, and it will come in the next generation to Singapore as well.

The key imperative in the near term is to work to reform and consolidate the democracies that have emerged during the third wave—the majority of which remain illiberal and unstable, if they remain democratic at all. With more focused, committed, and resourceful international engagement, it should be possible to help democracy sink deeper and more enduring roots in countries such as Indonesia, the Philippines, South Africa, and Ghana. It is possible and urgently important to help stabilize the new democracies in Ukraine and Tunisia (whose success could gradually generate significant diffusion effects throughout the Arab world). It might be possible to nudge Thailand and Bangladesh back toward electoral democracy, though ways must be found to temper the awful levels of party polarization in each country. With time, the electoral authoritarian project in Turkey will discredit itself in the face of mounting corruption and abuse of power, which are already growing quite serious. And the oil-based autocracies in Iran and Venezuela will face increasingly severe crises of economic performance and political legitimacy.

It is vital that democrats in the established democracies not lose faith. Democrats have the better set of ideas. Democracy may be receding somewhat in practice, but it is still globally ascendant in peoples' values and aspirations. This creates significant new opportunities for democratic growth. If the current modest recession of democracy spirals into a depression, it will be because those of us in the established democracies were our own worst enemies.

NOTES

The author would like to thank Erin Connors, Emmanuel Ferrario, and Lukas Friedemann for their excellent research assistance on this essay.

1. For an elaboration of this definition, see Larry Diamond, *The Spirit of Democracy: The Struggle to Build Free Societies Throughout the World* (New York: Times Books, 2008), 20–26.
2. Steven Levitsky and Lucan Way, *Competitive Authoritarianism: Hybrid Regimes after the Cold War* (New York: Cambridge University Press, 2010); see also their essay in this volume.
3. I count as liberal democracies all those regimes that receive a score of 1 or 2 (out of 7) on *both* political rights and civil liberties.
4. Thomas Carothers, "The End of the Transition Paradigm," *Journal of Democracy* 13 (January 2002): 5–21.
5. Freedom House classifies all the world's regimes as democracies or not from 1989 to the present based on whether (a) they score at least 7 out of 12 on the "electoral process" dimension of political rights; (b) they score at least 20 out of 40 overall on the raw point scale for political rights; (c) their most recent parliamentary and presidential elections

were reasonably free and fair; (d) there are no significant hidden sources of power overriding the elected authorities; and (e) there are no recent legal changes abridging future electoral freedom. In practice, this has led to a somewhat expansive list of democracies—rather too generous in my view, but at least a plausible "upper limit" of the number of democracies every year. Levitsky and Way suggest in Chapter Four of this volume that a better standard for democracy would be the Freedom House classification of Free, which requires a minimum average score of 2.5 on the combined scales of political rights and civil liberties. But I think this standard excludes many genuine but illiberal democracies.

6. My count of electoral democracies for 1998–2002 was lower than that of Freedom House by 8 to 9 countries, and in 1999, by 11 countries. For example, I dropped from this category Georgia in 1992–2002, Ukraine in 1994–2004, Mozambique in 1994–2008, Nigeria in 1999–2003, Russia in 2001–4, and Venezuela in 2004–8.
7. Amy R. Poteete, "Democracy Derailed? Botswana's Fading Halo," *AfricaPlus*, 20 October 2014, *http://africaplus.wordpress.com/2014/10/20/democracy-derailed-botswanas-fading-halo/.*
8. Levitsky and Way, *Competitive Authoritarianism*, 20.
9. Kenneth Good, "The Illusion of Democracy in Botswana," in Larry Diamond and Marc F. Plattner, eds., *Democratization in Africa: Progress and Retreat*, 2nd ed. (Baltimore: Johns Hopkins University Press, 2010), 281.
10. The comparisons here and in figure 2 are with the reconfigured political-rights and civil-liberties scales, after the subscales for transparency and rule of law have been removed (see note 11 below).
11. I created the scale of transparency and rule of law by drawing subscales C2 (control of corruption) and C3 (accountability and transparency) from the political-rights scale and the four subscales of F (rule of law) from the civil-liberties scale. For the specific items in these subscales, see the Freedom in the World methodology, *www.freedomhouse.org/report/freedom-world-2014/methodology#.VGww5vR4qcI.*
12. Francis Fukuyama, *Political Order and Political Decay: From the Industrial Revolution to the Globalization of Democracy* (New York: Farrar, Straus & Giroux, 2014). See also his essay in this volume.
13. On Russia, see Miriam Lanskoy and Elspeth Suthers, "Putin versus Civil Society: Outlawing the Opposition," *Journal of Democracy* 24 (July 2013): 74–87.
14. See Andrew Nathan's essay, "China's Challenge," on pp. 156–70 in the twenty-fifth anniversary issue of the *Journal of Democracy*.

15. Christopher Walker and Robert W. Orttung, "Breaking the News: The Role of State-Run Media," *Journal of Democracy* 25 (January 2014): 71–85.
16. Carl Gershman and Michael Allen, "The Assault on Democracy Assistance," *Journal of Democracy* 17 (April 2006): 36–51; William J. Dobson, *The Dictator's Learning Curve: Inside the Global Battle for Democracy* (New York: Doubleday, 2012).
17. Darin Christensen and Jeremy M. Weinstein, "Defunding Dissent: Restrictions on Aid to NGOs," *Journal of Democracy* 24 (April 2013): 77–91.
18. See the essays in Larry Diamond and Marc F. Plattner, *Liberation Technology: Social Media and the Struggle for Democracy* (Baltimore: John Hopkins University Press, 2012) and the ongoing trailblazing work of the Citizen Lab, *https://citizenlab.org/*.

ABOUT THE AUTHORS

Thomas Carothers is vice-president for studies at the Carnegie Endowment for International Peace and the author, most recently, of *Development Aid Confronts Politics: The Almost Revolution* (with Diane de Gramont, 2013) and *Closing Space: Democracy and Human Rights Support under Fire* (with Saskia Brechenmacher, 2014).

Larry Diamond is founding coeditor of the *Journal of Democracy*, senior fellow at the Hoover Institution and the Freeman Spogli Institute for International Studies at Stanford University, and director of Stanford's Center on Democracy, Development, and the Rule of Law.

Francis Fukuyama is the Olivier Nomellini senior fellow at the Center on Democracy, Development, and the Rule of Law at Stanford. His most recent book is *Political Order and Political Decay: From the Industrial Revolution to the Globalization of Democracy* (2014).

Robert Kagan is senior fellow with the Project on International Order and Strategy at the Brookings Institution in Washington, DC. His books include *The World America Made* (2012) and *The Return of History and the End of Dreams* (2008).

Steven Levitsky is professor of government at Harvard University. He is the coauthor, with Lucan Way, of *Competitive Authoritarianism: Hybrid Regimes after the Cold War* (2010), and the coeditor, with Kenneth M. Roberts, of *The Resurgence of the Latin American Left* (2011).

Marc F. Plattner is founding coeditor of the *Journal of Democracy*, vice-president for research and studies at the National Endowment for Democracy (NED), and co-chair of the Research Council of NED's International Forum for Democratic Studies.

Philippe C. Schmitter, professor emeritus in the Department of Political and Social Sciences at the European University Institute, previously taught at the University of Chicago and Stanford University. He is the coeditor (with Guillermo O'Donnell and Laurence Whitehead) of the seminal four-volume series *Transitions from Authoritarian Rule*.

Lucan Way is associate professor of political science at the University of Toronto. He is the coauthor, with Steven Levitsky, of *Competitive Authoritarianism: Hybrid Regimes after the Cold War* (2010), and author of *Pluralism by Default and the Rise of Competitive Politics after the Cold War* (forthcoming).

INDEX